# THE RIVER RUNS RED

Mark Bridgeman

Watermill Books

Published in 2019 by

Watermill Books
Mill Street
Aberfeldy
Perthshire PH15 2BG
www.aberfeldywatermill.com

British Library Cataloguing-in-Publication Data

A catalogue record for this book is available from the British Library

ISBN 978-0-9957795-1-8

Designed by EMB Graphics, Aberfeldy

Printed and bound in the UK by Bell and Bain Ltd, Glasgow

# THE RIVER RUNS RED

Mark Bridgeman

Illustrated by Elaine Dunsmore

Watermill Books

# CONTENTS

# INTRODUCTION
# SCRATCHING THE SURFACE

A journey from Killin, travelling alongside the loch and then following the River Tay to where it meets the River Tummel near Pitlochry, takes in one of the most tranquil settings in Scotland. Tree-lined hills to the north and south, capped with snow in winter, make for a beautiful backdrop to the area's picturesque towns and villages: Kenmore, Grandtully and Aberfeldy to the west, to the North Pitlochry and Kinloch Rannoch, with Dunkeld nestled to the south.

Yet the beauty of Highland Perthshire and the majesty of the River Tay conceal a dark past with a catalogue of murderous crime and unsolved mysteries. The Tower Cottage murder in 1947 brought national attention and a police manhunt. Looking further back, there are some crimes that today would not even be considered offences, yet at that time warranted penal servitude or transportation to the colonies. Meanwhile other serious crimes, sometimes even those including murder, were treated more lightly that we might expect, with 'the drink' often seen as mitigating circumstance.

Unsolved mysteries that perhaps, will never be unravelled and missing bodies never found - there is a touch of tragedy, of comedy, of mystery and even of the supernatural. Crimes of self-preservation, of greed and of revenge. Offences often caused, or exacerbated, by poverty, desperation, ignorance, mental illness and drink. Some cases were resolved, some will always remain an enigma. In the days before DNA and forensic science, the chances of a perpetrator being apprehended were usually very low.

In researching this book, the most startling revelation was the number of unsolved mysteries to occur within Highland Perthshire during the past 200 years. There have been countless stories of people 'gone a-missing', with no credible reason given.

Families and the newspapers reported case after case of missing persons. There was obviously a concerted effort to reduce public levels of fear, as those missing were reported as "drowned by accident", "lost their way in the dark", or "suffering from a loss of memory".

While tragic accidents do occur, the nineteenth century crime figures suggest an almost lawless state existing on Perthshire's roads, especially prior to the existence of a local police force, backed up by telephone and telegraph. Locals walking the country roads, especially at night, lived in genuine and constant fear of being robbed by groups of vagabonds and itinerants who often camped in the region.

This collection only scratches the surface - there are many more unsolved cases and mysteries, enough to fill another book!

Perhaps the real interest in some of the stories presented here is that we can never fully know the circumstances, leaving our imaginations to create the conclusions we desire.


Mark Bridgeman

# 6:16AM: THE MYSTERIOUS DISAPPEARANCE OF JOHN CRERAR

Early on the morning of Thursday 17th September 1925, John Crerar carefully closed the front door of his home at Bridgend in Aberfeldy. It was 6am and he did not wish to disturb his widowed mother, with whom he lived. The sun had not yet risen and the street was quiet, except for a few men also on their way to work. John, aged 27, had already worked at McGrouthers, the butchers in Dunkeld Street, for many years and set off to walk the few hundred yards to the shop, as he had done on many occasions. He was never seen alive again.

John's mother, Mrs Carmichael, rose an hour or so later, dressed, and made her own way to McGrouthers to make some purchases. She knew she would be able to speak to John in the shop, as she had always done. It was just after 8am when she entered the premises.

Mr McGrouther greeted her with some surprise: "Is there anything wrong with John this morning?", he enquired, "he has not turned up for work".

"That's funny", she replied, "he left for work as usual at six o'clock this morning".

Mrs Carmichael rushed home. John's room appeared as it should. As far as she could ascertain, he had left for work in the morning. His work clothes were gone, although he did not appear to have taken any money with him. Worried, she went to look for John but could find no trace of him. The local police were informed and a search party was organised. Sergeant McFarlane and Constable Smart circulated a description which was printed in the local press:

## MISSING ABERFELDY MAN

*The missing man is about 5ft 8in in height, of ordinary build, with fresh to dark complexion, and black hair. When he left his home he was dressed in a dark grey jacket and vest, brown tweed trousers, and a grey cap.*

The disappearance was a complete mystery. John was quiet, likeable and hard working. He had been a shop assistant at McGrouthers for many years, starting as a boy before the Great War. During the conflict he had volunteered for the Black Watch Regiment, and had seen active service in France, Egypt and Salonica. After the armistice he returned to work at McGrouthers, but he suffered a great deal from recurrent attacks of malaria fever. He had been a reliable employee, was popular, and had many friends.

Searches were carried out all across the valley, in the

countryside and in the town. Friends of John even organised their own search. The Tay river had been swollen by recent heavy rainfall but a search was carried out, both along the banks and in the water (using special water glasses to aid underwater vision).

Their efforts were fruitless and puzzling. The police were surprised that – although it was quiet on the streets at that time of the morning – not a single person could recall seeing him or noticing anything unusual. John's disappearance was out of character and both his mother and employer could not imagine any possible reason for the mystery.

It had been mentioned that he suffered recurrences of the malaria he had contracted while on active service - however it was odd that no witnesses could recall seeing anybody in difficulty or behaving strangely.

One week passed and despite intensive efforts by the police and family, not a single clue to John's disappearance had surfaced. *The Dundee Courier* and *Perthshire Advertiser* newspapers repeated the family's plea for information, and the missing man's photograph was circulated widely.

How could a man completely vanish between two buildings just a few hundred yards apart? It was surmised that perhaps he had suffered a loss of memory, and was wandering, hopelessly lost somewhere.

Another week passed and the recent wet weather had receded. On the evening of Saturday 3rd October, Mr

James Aird (a road roller engine driver with Perthshire
County Council) decided to go fishing in an area of
the River Tay, known locally as the Toll Pool. Around
6.30pm he made a tragic discovery when he noticed
what appeared to be a body floating in the river. He
immediately informed Sergeant McFarlane who, along
with several others, managed to recover the body from
the water. It was immediately identified as that of John
Crerar, and taken to the ambulance station at the
Aberfeldy Town Hall. The funeral was arranged and
took place at Kenmore Parish Church a few days later.
Yet the question of what happened to John Crerar
was never properly answered. How did a quiet and
popular young man who had left his home, heading
for work, end up in the River Tay approximately three
quarters of a mile away?

The Moness Burn runs under the road, in close
proximity to the Crerar household. This burn then
runs into the Tay. However, the burn is surrounded
by a wall and he could not have possibly fallen in by
accident. He would, in any case, have been well aware
of its presence. The burn, along with the river, had
been thoroughly searched during the previous two
weeks. Although the burn had been swollen by the
recent heavy rain, it seems unlikely it could carry a
body as far as the river.

If he had suddenly been taken ill, why did nobody
notice him? If he had passed out, why was his
unconscious body not spotted by a passer-by? If he had
temporarily felt unwell, why not just return home?

After all, his home was very close by.

The weather is still mild in mid-September, so he was unlikely to have succumbed to the cold.

John Crerar had exhibited no sign of being agitated or depressed. Yet, if he had intended to end his own life, why get up early, dress for work and leave the house with no deviation from his usual routine?

If something more sinister had been the motive, it would have required a person or persons unknown to have lain in wait and either forced, or lured, their victim to his watery grave. His clothing contained no money, yet his wristwatch was still on his arm. It appeared that his body had been in the water since the day of his disappearance (despite the thorough search of the river) and little could be deduced from an examination. John Crerar's mother did not think he had taken any money with him, however she could not be certain. His routine was well known, as he left for the butchers at the same time every day. Yet there were no reports of any suspicious people near his house. In fact, no witnesses could be found at all. His route to work required just a simple walk through The Square and into Dunkeld Street, a walk of just two or three minutes.

The police could only be certain of one thing in the whole perplexing and tragic mystery. John Crerar's watch had stopped at 6:16am, just 16 minutes after he had left the house and – it was assumed - his body had entered the water.

After the burial, Sergeant McFarlane, armed with a stopwatch, decided to pace out the journey from the Crerar house at Bridgend to the nearest point in the river. The journey took him exactly 16 minutes.

# THE ONE-ARMED MAN
# AND THE LOCKED ROOM

On the night of 4th October 1921, a tense drama
played itself out on the West Moulin Road in Pitlochry.
The setting was a fine Victorian villa with spacious
grounds fringed with trees, plants and bushes. The
frontage, with its three gabled windows and wooden
framed porch, commanded a view to the south east,
across the town.

Mrs Christina Robertson, a widow, had settled into her
bed for the night in one of the bedrooms on the first
floor. In a bedroom across the landing slept her young
daughter and her daughter's friend, who happened
to be visiting for the night. All the lamps had been
dimmed. The family's small dog, Pax, was asleep
downstairs. Jessie Robertson (no relation), the family's
maid, occupied a small room on the ground floor.

At 4am Mrs Robertson was suddenly woken from her
slumber by the sound of screaming from downstairs.
This was immediately followed by hurried footsteps
on the staircase. Mrs Robertson's first thought was
for her daughter and rushed to open the panelled

door of her bedroom. On doing so, she was shocked to see her maid Jessie running towards her, one hand clutching a wound on her throat. The maid, hysterical, screamed "there's a man downstairs, and he's attacked me". Her throat was cut and was bleeding profusely. Jessie's garments were stained and vivid red. Mrs Robertson, showing remarkable courage and presence of mind, rushed across the landing and quickly hastened her daughter and friend back into her own room. Fortunately, as was the custom in large Victorian houses, the bedroom doors were all of the lockable variety. Quickly, Mrs Robertson turned the key and locked the door from the inside. In the height of the commotion, they could not detect the sound of the mysterious assailant on the stairs, although the small dog was barking incessantly from somewhere on the floor below.

After securing the bedroom door she was able to assess the extent of the wound to Jessie's throat. Although she did not think it was life threatening, it would definitely require hospital attention. However, they could not possibly unlock the door and make their way downstairs. Was the unknown man still in the house? Or had he made his way outside? Pax was still barking. Meanwhile the young girls had remained remarkably calm, and managed to console Jessie, the maid. Mrs Robertson knew they would not be able to jump, or climb, from the upstairs window sill, particularly with two small girls and her maid injured and bleeding. Then she remembered, she had kept a whistle in the

drawer of her dressing table.
She quickly raised the sash
window at the front and
began to blow the whistle
as often, and as loudly, as
she could. The shrill sound
echoed around the trees and
pierced the dark night. Would
the sound alert the intruder, or
would it frighten him away? Mrs

Robertson had no way of knowing, but she continued
to blow frantically, hoping someone would hear her
cry for help.

It must have been an anxious vigil in the locked
bedroom, as it was fully 45 minutes until help
came. Several times Mrs Robertson had thought
about unlocking the bedroom door and venturing
downstairs. She knew Jessie, her servant, needed
medical attention but was fully aware that the intruder
may still be in the house. Eventually, just before 5am,
a neighbour woken by the constant sound of the
whistle decided to investigate. She hurriedly dressed
and immediately ventured outside onto the street. As
her eyes became accustomed to the faint light of early
morning, she was met by sight of a "strange looking"
one armed man, obviously leaving from the back of
the villa, then attempting to make his way down the
road. The man was thick set, clean shaven and about
40 years of age. Immediately, fearing something was
amiss, she challenged him:

"Who are you, and what do you want?" she demanded.

To her astonishment he replied; "Which is the way to the police station?".

The neighbour was somewhat surprised by the answer and, thinking it to be an attempt to throw her off the scent, repeated her demand:

"What are you doing here?" she again asked.

"I want the police station" came the answer.

During this strange encounter Mrs Robertson was still blowing the whistle and the dog still barking. Worrying that something sinister may be happening in the house, the neighbour hastily directed the sturdily built one armed man to the police station. He duly disappeared into the early morning mist. Now, joined by another neighbour, (a stonemason on his way to work) the pair rushed through the open back door into the kitchen. The light was burning and a broken cut-throat razor lay on the floor. There were traces of blood.

Hearing voices in the house calling out "What is the matter?", Mrs Robertson unlocked the bedroom door and appeared on the landing. The local doctor was called and Jessie's wounds attended to. She was removed to the Pitlochry Cottage Hospital. Meanwhile the local police were summoned, who immediately engaged the help of the Procurator Fiscal for Perthshire, to investigate the case. The Procurator Fiscal's office, in Scotland, is the body appointed to investigate serious crime.

The bizarre events of the night had thrown up several mysteries. Who was the one-armed man? Why had he attacked the maid, Jessie? Was theft a motive? Had he been disturbed? Why did the one-armed man want to know the location of the police station? Did he intend to hand himself in, or was it merely a distraction to put the neighbours at their ease?

Some puzzling questions immediately occurred to the investigating officers. There were no signs of forced entry into the house and the downstairs lights were on. Why would a man choose to break into a house in which the occupants were clearly awake? Would not a one-armed man find it difficult to effect a forcible entry into a home anyway? If the intruder had been a burglar, then the cut-throat razor (found broken on the floor) was an odd choice of weapon and not really a suitable one to help with a robbery.

A search of the maid's room also revealed some other telling clues. Upon her return from the cottage hospital Jessie, the maid, was questioned thoroughly. In the meantime, the mysterious one armed man had, indeed, wanted the local police station in Pitlochry. Shortly after the attack he had calmly entered the station and handed himself in.

David McDougall, a painter's labourer who gave his address as 1, Church Place, Edinburgh, pleaded guilty to a charge of "stabbing or cutting Jessie Robertson with a razor on the throat, with the intent to murder her, or maim and disfigure her". He was remanded to Perth Prison pending further inquiries.

The evidence of Jessie Robertson, the maid, was sought and a special sitting of the High Court in Perth was called for Monday 21st November 1921. Lord Blackburn, KC presided, with Mr DP Fleming, KC prosecuting for the Crown and Mr T Grainger Stewart acting for the defence.

Following a prayer from the Rev JM Scott (the traditional way to open proceedings) the indictment was read to the packed courtroom:

*On October 4th, in a house known as Woodsheil, occupied by Mrs Christina Robertson, he did assault Jessie Robertson, residing there, and did cut her on the neck and shoulder with a razor, and did attempt to murder her.*

David McDougall pled guilty initially to just an attempt to commit bodily harm, but on advice, admitted guilt to all the charges. Mr Fleming began his case for the prosecution with the stunning evidence of Jessie Robertson. From information given to the prosecution by the maid, it was revealed that she was, in fact, the sister of Mr McDougall's wife. The accused had a relationship with his wife's sister, even spending time living with her on occasion. Without his wife's knowledge and without the knowledge of Mrs Robertson, Jessie's employer, he had been living in Woodsheil. In fact, for the three days prior to the attack he had been sharing Jessie's bedroom at the house, without the knowledge of her employer. Just how this was accomplished, without Mrs Robertson being alerted, must have required much cunning and stealth on the part of the illicit pair.

On the night of the attack McDougall admitted that he had been drinking, and it is believed an argument between the couple ensued. What was the violent disagreement between the pair? Perhaps one of them wanted to end the affair? Perhaps Jessie had threatened to tell her sister? Perhaps McDougall, in a moment of guilt, had confessed to his wife? The reason was never revealed.

However, the accused, thanks to a robust defence by Mr Grainger Stewart, appeared a much more sympathetic figure than the victim, Jessie Robertson. McDougall, the court was told, had been in the army and served his country in India until 1909 when he suffered an unfortunate accident, resulting in the loss of his arm. He was subsequently discharged from the army and fell into bad company, at which point he began drinking heavily. He admitted that at the time of the assault he was "muddled with drink", rather than being "drunk". Mr Grainger Stewart told the court that McDougall was not "such a wicked criminal as one who would commit an assault in cold blood".

It is interesting to note just how often, during the 19th and early 20th Century, that an over-indulgence in alcohol was seen as a mitigating circumstance and not a contributory factor in serious criminal cases!

The defence was also able to show that it would be a difficult thing for a one-armed man to murderously attack a victim, since he would require one hand to brandish the weapon and the other to restrain the victim. This might perhaps explain why Jessie Robertson was able to escape the attack and make her way upstairs.

Lord Blackburn also noted that the injuries to the woman were not as serious as had first been thought and, in fact, although justifiably frightened, she might well have exaggerated the seriousness of the assault. The court had no witnesses, other than the victim herself, to the murderous intent of the attack. Perhaps, in an effort to maintain her employment, she had embellished her claim?

The seriousness of an attack with a razor was rightly taken into account, together with the prisoner's plea of guilty, and McDougall was sentenced to 3 years' penal servitude (prison with hard labour).

It is worth noting that assaults with cut-throat razors were far more commonplace a century ago than they are today. This type of razor was an everyday item, and therefore the attack did not carry the "shock" value that perhaps it would today.

Penal servitude was considered a harsher punishment than a normal custodial sentence as the work enforced on the prisoner was often pointless, unpaid, harsh and uncompromising. This type of sentence was abolished in Scotland in 1950, following the Criminal Justice (Scotland) Act 1949.

# LAST SEEN AT KILLIN

On the morning of Saturday 15th October 1892, Mr Charles William Lambe Forbes could be seen walking briskly westward from Aberfeldy, on the road towards Kenmore. Although the morning was pleasant, Mr Forbes was carrying his Ulster coat, guarding against the possibility of rain. With the heavy Donegal tweed coat over his arm and carrying a small document case in the other hand, Forbes left the last houses of Aberfeldy behind and walked along the narrow, tree lined, winding road.

Charles Forbes was a distinguished gentleman, in his mid-60s, and well respected in the town. Liked for his genial manner and social nature, Forbes was an agent for the Commercial Bank of Aberfeldy, and a practising solicitor, as well as running a coal and manure business and acting as a Commissioner for the Inland Revenue. His status within the town had also brought with it a seat on the School Board, Justice of the Peace, Chief Magistrate and the town's representative on the Perth County Council.

As Charles Forbes was just reaching the edge of

Aberfeldy, he passed one of his sons coming in
the other direction with his horse and wagonette.
Surprised at seeing his father walking in the direction
of Kenmore, he enquired as to his destination. His
father replied, stating that he had business in Killin.
His son offered to turn around and drive him. Charles
Forbes declined, saying he would continue walking
until the Kenmore bound stagecoach passed him.
After jumping on board the Kenmore coach, he
explained to his son, he intended to alight at Kenmore
Pier and catch the 12.40pm Loch Tay steamer to Killin.
His son, satisfied by the explanation, continued into
town.  Charles Forbes did exactly as he had detailed
to his son. After hailing the stagecoach he got off at
Kenmore and boarded the Loch Tay steamer, Lady of
The Lake, purchasing a five shilling return ticket. After
a pleasant journey on the attractive vessel, with its pine
planking and teakwood hatchways and fittings, Forbes
disembarked at Killin Pier and caught the connecting
train at Killin Pier Railway Station, heading for Killin
Junction Station. Once there he could travel either
east or west on the Callander And Oban Railway.  On
arriving at Killin Junction Station, Forbes handed in
his ticket.

There were two trains in the station, waiting at the
platform, under the attractive white footbridge.
One was heading east to Oban and the other west to
Callander. No one at the station remembered which
train Charles Forbes boarded (or even if he boarded a
train at all). He was never seen again.

His complete disappearance raised eyebrows locally.
What could have happened to this genial pillar of
Aberfeldy society? Charles Forbes's business matters
were left unattended. Days passed into weeks. Mr Reid,
the bank's accountant, took temporary charge at the
Commercial Bank in Aberfeldy, and junior magistrates
were forced to chair commissioner's meetings in the
town. Rumours began to circulate throughout the
town. Forbes's first wife's family lived in America, and
it was widely conjectured that he had travelled there.
Perhaps taking the westbound train from Killin and
catching a steamer from one of the west coast ports.
His eldest daughter, Susie, was due to be married in
Bombay, India, however, there is no record of him
attending the wedding. Besides, sailing times to India
in the 1890s would not have allowed him to reach
Bombay in time for the ceremony. Whatever would
make a respectable and well liked local businessman

leave everything behind and simply vanish? The town wanted answers, the Town Council grew increasingly worried – for they knew the reason why.

As a matter of good business practice and due diligence, the Commercial Bank ordered a complete audit of the Aberfeldy Branch's books and cash reserves. Everything was found to be in good order.

With no sign of Charles Forbes returning and no trace, word, or sighting, the Aberfeldy Town Council could wait no longer. An emergency meeting was called, and the full story would finally emerge.

A meeting of the Aberfeldy Town Council was held in January 1893. Charles Forbes's whereabouts were still unknown. The evening opened, not with the reading of the minutes from the previous meeting, but with the minutes from a special financial meeting, of the Council's Bell Fund Committee, held in 1876, some 17 years earlier. It was revealed that the Town Council had approved a 10-year secured loan from the Bell Fund to Forbes's elder brother, Dr JTG Forbes. The bond had been secured against the family's estate, Auchrannie, near Forfar (The scheme, designed to assist recipients in making large scale investment, thus assisting the local economy, returned a dividend of 2 -3% in interest to the coffers of the Council). Unfortunately, the bond had become due in 1886. As several members of the Town Council engaged in an undignified scramble to deflect blame from themselves, the amount of the original loan to the Forbes family in 1876 was revealed – a staggering £4,000 (today's equivalent being almost half a million pounds!). The loan had been secured on the Auchrannie Estate, which Dr Forbes had purchased for £3,120 a few years previously. He had also informed the committee that in excess of £2,000 had been spent on improving Auchrannie. Therefore, it was generally considered to be a worthwhile risk for the Bell Fund committee.

However, a problem arose as the due date for the repayment of the loan arrived in 1886. Dr Forbes, at that point was still alive and comfortably well off. It was claimed, at the Council meeting, that if he had been given adequate notice, either some, or all, of the outstanding monies could have been repaid. Instead, the bond was not collected, and the debt allowed to accrue. After the death of Dr Forbes Auchrannie passed over to Charles Forbes. The Town Council proposed that no action be taken, on seeking repayment of the loan in 1887, again in 1888, and every subsequent year until 1892. A valuation of the estate was estimated, in a report for the Council, at £6,000, which seemed to offer the members some comfort. For the time being, at least, their security seemed safe.

With the sudden disappearance of Charles Forbes tensions were running high. Property and land values had reduced by as much as 30-40% between 1880 and 1892. This, in turn, had suppressed agricultural prices, making the Council's valuation, at best, unreliable, at worst, hugely optimistic.

As the weeks turned into months, a sequestration

order was sought over the Auchrannie estate. Bankruptcy proceedings were held on 27th March 1893 at the Sheriff's Court in Perth – in Charles Forbes's absence – and a trustee was appointed. Auchrannie was sold in a bankruptcy auction held on 21st April, at which Mr D McDiarmid (an agent acting on behalf of an unknown client) purchased the estate for £900. Proceeds of the sale were to be distributed to creditors, once all the assets of Charles Forbes had been realised.

It was reported later in the year that the Dowager-Countess of Airlie had purchased the estate, primarily as Auchrannie bordered her own estate in the Den of Airlie. The cost reported at that time was a little over £2,000, perhaps indicating that not all the land and assets were included in the original price of £900.

Creditors (including the Aberfeldy Town Council) were paid a dividend from the sale proceeds at two appointed meetings, both held at the Breadalbane Arms Hotel, on 12th June 1894 and 22nd March 1895. With Charles Forbes still in absentia, full repayment of the outstanding bond would never materialise, leaving Aberfeldy Town Council battered and financially bruised. Further minutes of Council meetings show that the original approval of the loan received unanimous support, leaving no individual to take responsibility for the deficit.

As for Charles Forbes? There is a record of a Charles Forbes sailing from Glasgow for New York in 1892. Did he live out the remaining years of his life in the USA, or perhaps join his newly married daughter's family in India? All we can say for sure is that Aberfeldy Town Council drew a hasty and slightly embarrassed veil over proceedings.

# THE DUNKELD RIOTS

A group of travellers, camping in the Inver Woods near Dunkeld, were awoken early in the morning of 6th September 1869 by an explosion. The loud noise, likened to an echoing gunshot, caused the ground to shudder, as if an imaginary underground tunnel had collapsed.

Nearby, smoke could be seen spiralling upwards from the trees surrounding the Falls above the River Braan, at which was located the ornate Ossian's Hall. The structure, built by the then Duke of Atholl, was ornate and extravagant. Built to showcase the falls in all their glory, the building (also known locally as The Hermitage) was situated on the rocky banks above the Braan, nestling between a cluster of trees, and sat 40 feet above the river. Ossian's Hall, part of the Duke of Atholl's Dunkeld estate, welcomed its visitors through an ornate wooden door featuring an inlaid oil painting. As the visitor passed through, the door slid into a recess, rather than swing open on hinges. Once inside, any guest of the Duke would pass into the saloon, a dome roofed room featuring a marble floor, fine furniture and many richly gilded mirrors, which lined the walls and ceiling. At the far end of the room, a finely formed bow window afforded a breathtaking view of the foaming and rushing Braan below.

In the early hours of the morning the Police Sergeant from Dunkeld investigated the source of the explosion. As he reached the site of Ossian's Hall a scene of devastation greeted him. A section of the stone walls and roof had been blown away by the explosion (inside, what remained of the hall, nothing had survived). The ornate roofing and lathing had been destroyed. Debris was scattered over a wide area. The gilded mirrors and furniture were completely gone. Literally blown to smithereens. The smell of gunpowder still filled the room.

Mr Melville Jameson, the Procurator Fiscal for the County of Perthshire, was summoned. Immediately, it was deduced that a side door had been used to force an entry. One, or possibly two barrels of gunpowder had been dragged inside the building, and a fuse trail created which led away from the hall.

Despite Dunkeld's tranquil setting at the gateway to the Highlands, this was not the first act of what would now be called 'terrorism' to take place in the town. Just six days earlier, 12 spruce trees on the Duke of Atholl's property had been set alight. A reward of £25 (£3,000 today) had already been offered, by the authorities, to catch the perpetrators. Agitation within the town had reached such fever pitch, during the past year, that the English newspapers had dubbed Dunkeld the "Tipperary of Scotland" in reference to the anti-establishment activities taking place in Ireland.

The reason for the deliberate bombing of The
Hermitage was, on the face of it, a surprising one
- the construction of the famous Thomas Telford
designed bridge in the town. Construction costs of
the stone bridge were estimated at £15,000 in 1809.

A government grant of £7,500 was obtained, with the
town bearing the remainder of the cost. However,
the estimate proved unreliable as costs spiralled to
£40,000. The Duke of Atholl agreed to finance the
shortfall, with an agreement that a toll could be levied
to help recuperate his costs. Tollgates were erected
across the bridge, with access to the other side not
permitted until the toll was paid. Tolls were extremely
unpopular in Victorian Britain. Seen as a tax on the
poor, tempers ran high in Dunkeld. Agitators among
the local population organised periodic riots, during
which the tollgates were removed and thrown into
the river. The seriousness of the disturbances caused
the local authorities to build the local jail under the
bridge, on the Dunkeld side. The door can still be
seen today.

A month before the destruction of The Hermitage, an attempt to destroy the tollgates and tollhouse, in similar circumstances, had been thwarted. A trail of gunpowder had been discovered leading to the tollhouse, and the conspirators were frightened off. Perhaps they had considered that an attack on Ossian's Hall would be far more likely to succeed.

There were many attempts to destroy the tollgates and many riots, involving mobs descending on the bridge, violence and civil disobedience. Perhaps the worst occurred between 10th-12th July 1868, when an angry mob stormed the bridge and, due to strength of numbers, managed to rip the east tollgate from its foundations, including the supports and railings. The collection box was smashed and the Tollhouse was surrounded, the occupants terrorised, and the windows smashed. A group of law-abiding locals, marshalled by local Police Constables Masson and Low, attempted to confront the mob and were viciously attacked. Iron spars ripped from the tollgate were used to attack the Constables and reinforcements were called for. Arrests followed and the main antagonists were tried at the High Court of The Justiciary in Perth. Prison sentences for "mobbing and rioting" were dispensed to the main agitators, Daniel Blair (labourer), Henry Scott (carter) and John Fraser (shoemaker), all residents of Dunkeld.

The attack on Ossian's Hall was traced to George Campbell, a quarrier known to have expertise with gunpowder. Campbell was known locally to vehemently oppose tolls on the bridge. He was arrested and charged.

A proposed visit of Queen Victoria to The Hermitage (a favourite spot of Her Majesty during visits to Scotland) was postponed.

Despite the arrest and imprisonment of the main offenders, protests continued. Occasional riots and other forms of dissent would surface. A form of 'peaceful protest' became popular, in which a local resident would simply refuse to pay the toll and walk across the bridge, in collusion with a friendly tollkeeper, who would not collect a toll. Infuriated with this, the Duke of Atholl took several locals to court, citing their failure to pay. One such resident, a Mr Robertson, claimed he could not afford the toll, whilst under the threat of bankruptcy, but would be happy to pay once the threat had been lifted!

Letters were also written to the Scottish newspapers and to the council in Perth, urging the removal of the tolls.

Eventually, tiring of the endless expense and unrest, the County Roads Authority took over the running of the bridge in 1879. The tollgates and collection box were removed and Dunkeld became the peaceful and picturesque town it is today.

# WHISKY GALORE

Whisky, crime and tragedy seem to have a long relationship in Highland Perthshire. There has always been 'money in whisky', whether it be excise duty, avoiding paying excise duty, distilling, robbery or smuggling. Highland Perthshire has more than its fair share of stories.

From the mid 1750s barley was grown in considerable quantities in the valley, potatoes and turnips too. High freight costs to the cities made distilling a far more profitable option. Private stills were a common sight in caves and hollows on the hillsides, but often in the open glens. Conditions were ideal, with a plentiful supply of grain and clean spring water. Until 1814 small private stills were permitted, providing tax was paid. However, after that date, all legal distilling was subject to excise duty. The excise men visited the area often, looking to catch illegal operations. On arriving in the area, after a long journey, the excise party would invariably stop at a local hostelry for refreshment and to rest the horses. Their technique was to look for the smoke plumes from peat fires curling up through the grass and trees. Often their brief break for sustenance enabled local people to warn the distillers in time. Even the clergy were rumoured to be involved in the impressive early warning system.

Not all the illicit hooch was produced for local consumption. Much of it was smuggled south of the border in ingeniously designed containers. Examples included a 'belly canteen', worn under a woman's garments, to give the impression of advanced pregnancy. Or a special container, wrapped in a shawl and fake leather head, intended to look like a second passenger, riding on the back of the smuggler's horse.

From the hills above Loch Tay to the convergence of the Tay and Tummel rivers, stills were as widespread as the schemes used to throw the excise men off the scent.

Local tales tell of a farmer, on the hills above Loch Tay, near Lawers, who kept an illicit still, cunningly hidden in a hollow on the hillside. The excise officials sent by the Government were well aware of the existence of the still but, despite all their efforts, could not find it. The farmer would invite the excisemen into his home. On the pretence of offering to help them find the still, he would ply them with drink, spin them yarns regarding the possible site of a still, then send them on their merry way, hopelessly disorientated and nursing very sore heads!

Another story tells of a still located in a hollow in the hillside somewhere above Bolfracks, near Aberfeldy. The operators were approached in town by a gentleman, who wondered if they happened to know about the location of the still. Convinced that the gentleman was an excise official they offered to show him the exact spot, if he consented to being blindfolded. After a long and arduous trek, up and down hills, scrambling over rocks, and frequently changing direction, the gentleman found himself alone and completely lost, at the bottom of a ravine under a waterfall. Needless to say, there are no waterfalls on the Bolfracks hills.

The men from the excise did not give up easily, however. During the early 1800s they had become suspicious about the possible location of a still in a cottage, somewhere in Old Chapel Street in Aberfeldy. The owner, who openly sold his illicit whisky around the town for 1s 6d a gallon, became understandably worried. Fearing the worst, he packed all his distilling paraphernalia, together with a couple of barrels, onto a farm cart and headed into the countryside. After concealing his equipment at Callwood Cottage, near Coshieville, he then dumped the barrels in the river. Local rumours tell us that he never went back to recover them. Perhaps a lucky local chanced upon them, or perhaps they are still there, waiting to be discovered?

In fact, by the early nineteenth century the illegal
manufacturing of whisky (or 'smuggling') seems to
be have become the principal industry of Highland
Perthshire. As these reminiscences by Dr John
Kennedy, recalling his childhood in Aberfeldy during
the 1820s tell us, the risks and rewards from smuggling
were high:

*It was carried on in every glen and on every hillside,
and neither those who made nor those who drank the
whisky – these two classes comprising a very large part
of the population - thought this form of law-breaking at
all disreputable. General Stewart of Garth, whose riding
into Aberfeldy on his old grey Corunna Charger I well
remember, published in 1822 a considerable work on "The
Highlanders", in which he describes the general feeling of
disgust and indignation when landlord-magistrates inflicted
penalties for illicit distilling, seeing that the whisky thus
produced enabled the people to pay the landlords their rent;
considering also that freights to the lowlands were so high as
to prevent any legitimate profit being made from Highland
barley; and finally, that the illicit whisky was so much better
than that on which the King's duty had been paid!*

*The contest between exciseman and smuggler seems to have
been considered a sort of game in which either side was
entitled to any advantage it could score; for General Stewart
says that when the dragoons came raiding into the glens,
the smugglers, far from offering any resistance, showed true
Highland courtesy in inviting the raiders to partake of
refreshments, and even helped to destroy the implements of
their own trade when the destruction was inevitable. But this*

*I know well, that the smugglers used all their ingenuity to prevent discovery, and that their efforts were sympathised with and seconded by a large number of their fellow countrymen.*

*I remember one day when the troopers from Perth suddenly came over the hills and descended in force on Aberfeldy. Speedy as their movements were, the news of their invasion came faster than they did, and the consternation was as if the village was about to be besieged. Many of the people had illicit malt in their possession, and some of them came to my father begged for the keys of the chapel, feeling sure that if they could stow the malt there it would escape the house-to-house search that was sure to be made. My father had always set his face against smuggling and refused the key; but some of the malt was thrown over the fence into the chapel garden for sanctuary.*

*The Schoolmaster was not so scrupulous as the minister. In hot haste some bags full of malt were brought to the end of the schoolhouse, to its darkest part, and the boys, of whom I was one, were told to sit on them. Soon, Munro, the exciseman, accompanied by a soldier, came to the door and said- "Mr MacLean, have you anything in my line?" to which he replied there were none. They stepped in a foot or two, took a glance and went away, trusting to the dominee having told them the truth. A great deal of malt was seized in the village nevertheless, and about 200 sacks of the forbidden article were carted into Aberfeldy that day from various parts of the country round, under military escort. The exciseman, Munro, was nearly murdered by a detected smuggler, who was not quite as submissive as those described by General Stewart. The culprit, as this occasion, was sentenced to transportation.*

The efforts of the smugglers grew every more sophisticated, as did the exertions of the excisemen to find them. By the middle of the 19th Century an officer of the excise had taken a residence in the valley, much to the annoyance of the residents. The huge scale of the smuggling efforts continued, however. On 11th April 1845 two customs officials, Mr Donald Durran (the riding officer) and Mr William Lee (supervisor) discovered one of the most complete and comprehensive illegal operations for the "carrying on of illegal malting and distillation ever known in the country, all formed under the ground of a farm-steading in the neighbourhood of Aberfeldy". So complete was the facility that "they steeped, malted, dried and distilled in it". The smugglers had cunningly constructed, underneath a huge dung heap, a premises large underneath to complete all their operations underground, with a pipe connecting the vent from their still to a vent from a boiler some distance away, to give the appearance that the smoke plumes were, in fact, emanating from a boiler within the farm steading.

On another occasion Alexander Forbes, one of the best-known smugglers in the area, kept one of his many stills on the shores of Loch Glassie at the foot of Farragon Hill. He was surprised by a raid from the excisemen (or 'gaugers' as they were labelled locally). Forbes hurriedly picked up his pot still, badly burning his foot in the process, and waded into the Loch. He hoped to evade capture in the Loch and the cold water did, at least, numb the pain from his badly burned foot. A stand-off ensued, Forbes refused to leave the water until the excisemen departed. Although he escaped punishment on this occasion, he was confined to the house for six months due to the severity of his burns!

Following his recovery, he continued in his ventures until word reached him that he was wanted for trial on another count of smuggling. He was kept secretly hidden for a year until the warrant expired.

John Stewart, from Portnasallan near Grandtully, and Duncan Stewart, a blacksmith from Balnaguard, engaged in a profitable smuggling partnership. One day John Stewart was carrying a five-gallon cask of whisky, slung over his shoulder, concealed with a sack, to the inn at Guay. Unfortunately, the excisemen had become aware of his plans and lay in wait near the Inn. On seeing them, John dropped the cask hard on the road surface, hoping to – literally – wash away the evidence. The stout timbers of the cask, however, did not break and the Customs men seized both John and the whisky. Obviously in high spirits, they retired immediately to the Guay Inn and broached the cask. After several shots of the illicit spirit were shared, John was bound hand and foot and taken to the jail at Logierait. However, when friends of John's heard of the story, they threatened to expose the excisemen, effectively blackmailing them.

John was released and no charges were brought against him.

The pair were not always so lucky though. On one particularly unlucky day their three bothies, hidden on the mossy hillsides above Balnaguard, were found by the 'gaugers' and torched, including all their contents. To add insult to injury, all their possessions were taken and they were both fined the hefty sum of £3 10s (about £400 today).

During the late 1850s Duncan Thomson from the Braes of Grandtully Farm, together with friends, constructed an impressive still at an abandoned farmstead near Grandtully named Cor-an-easan. Underneath the courtyard of the farm they excavated a distilling operation complete with stone floor, wooden beams and clay plastered ceiling. A kiln and tank were vented via a concealed chimney. Unfortunately, despite their ingenious efforts, the still was discovered by eagle-eyed excisemen. Thomson was forced to flee the country for four years, taking his three sons with him. He returned in 1861, built and opened the Grandtully Hotel, which he operated until his retirement in 1897.

In Pitlochry a far more sophisticated and far reaching excise scam came to light in 1875. Following the chance discovery of a barrel of whisky on which duty had not been paid, aboard a train bound for Glasgow, excise officials became suspicious that further illicit barrels may have entered the market. An inspection was duly arranged for the Pitlochry Distillery, from where the barrel had begun its journey. Initial enquiries had revealed that a large number of barrels had left Pitlochry, bound for merchants and hotels, without the necessary duty paid.

On arriving at the Pitlochry Distillery, in the second week of October 1875, two Excise Inspector Generals inspected the distillery. The distillery had been inherited by Mrs Elizabeth Conacher in 1860 and was managed by her son Alexander. He welcomed the Inspectors to the distillery and, excusing himself, went to fetch all the company's business books. Nothing seemed amiss and the Inspectors were about to leave, ready to catch their train, when one of them suggested they should also check the bonded warehouse (a secured location where goods, liable for duty, are stored and strictly controlled). Once inside the warehouse, they resolved to test the casks. The first cask was opened and tasted. It contained water, and not whisky. They immediately tested a second one. It also contained just water. So did the third, and the fourth and the fifth. All told, more than 30 casks – which had contained whisky at the time of bonding – now contained only water.

The Inspectors were unable to work out how the whisky had been removed and replaced from what appeared to be a secured building. Alexander Conacher was immediately sent for. It transpired, however, that Conacher had picked up the distillery's business books and headed straight for the railway station. During the time the Inspectors were inside the premises, it was believed Conacher boarded a train headed south and absconded.

Under threat of prosecution, an employee of the
distillery gave the Inspectors the full story. A hole had
been made in the roof of the warehouse, through
which a person could slide through. The hole had
been designed so that it could be easily covered, thus
avoiding detection. The security bars were negotiated,
and the clandestine system of ingress and egress was
ready.  Once inside the warehouse, under cover of
night, a small, undetectable hole was made in one of
the side walls of the building. Meanwhile, outside the
warehouse, a large hole was dug in the undergrowth,
a large empty cask placed inside, and the hole covered
up. A syphon pipe was then connected from the cask
outside, passed through the hole in the wall, and the
syphoning of the whisky could begin. Once the whisky
had been safely removed, the process was reversed,
except the liquid syphoned back into the casks inside
the warehouse was water from the nearby burn.

The case attracted considerable publicity. Some of the
merchants who had received whisky from the Pitlochry
Distillery had not received their duty certification
from Alexander Conacher, and were liable for
prosecution. Even a cursory look at the Highland
Railway Company's books showed to just how many
destinations barrels of whisky had been travelling.
Those barrels that had been transported by road could
not be traced however, as Mr Conacher had vanished,
taking all the business books with him.

By December there was still no sign of Alexander
Conacher. All efforts to trace him had been fruitless. A

Justice of The Peace Court was convened in Perth, by Sheriff Barclay, and the true extent of the excise fraud came to light. As many as 60 firms had received casks from Conacher's but were still waiting for official duty paid certification. There may have been many more, but with the business records missing it was impossible to trace everyone involved. Many of those companies involved were fined for receiving "smuggled" whisky (despite Mr Conacher's promise that permits would be sent) and fined £12 10s.

So what did happen to the missing distillery manager? All efforts to contact him failed and it was thought by some that he may have taken his own life. There were even efforts, by certain merchants, to sue his estate for recompense.

It appeared that Mr Conacher was also a partner in another business, a grain manufacturers called Conacher & Harris. The company was badly in debt to the Caledonian Bank of Glasgow, among others. Total liabilities of £5,178 (£630,000 today) were offset by assets of £1,450. Clearly, desperate measures had been called for.

Creditors' meetings and bankruptcy proceedings followed in 1879 and the Pitlochry Distillery was sold to Peter Fraser & Co.

Mr Conacher does appear to have returned to Pitlochry, after the dust had settled. He seems to have been accepted back into the town's society, and was often seen at Highland Games, weddings and other social events. He passed away in 1899 and is buried at Moulin Parish Church (now the Moulin Heritage Centre).

By the beginning of the 20th Century the illegal distilling and smuggling of whisky had become less common. Hefty penalties acted as a deterrent. Any profits from the smuggling trade were swallowed up in the payment of fines. Several legal whisky distilleries were built in the area and these functioned as useful employers for previously 'self employed' distillers. They did, unfortunately, bring with them another crime that was to become associated with whisky – theft.

Improvements in motor cars, and to the Great North Road (now the A9), meant the opportunity now existed for thieves to arrive from other areas and help themselves to Highland Perthshire's most valuable commodity, whisky.

In September 1930 the Dalwhinne Distillery was robbed, under cover of darkness. Despite the presence of 12 staff in the main building and the nearby village, a small group of men silently managed to cut through the bars of a window belonging to the distillery's storeroom. Silently they syphoned 156 gallons of whisky into smaller containers. The theft was not discovered until the next morning when, judging by tyre marks and other tell-tale signs, the bandits (as they were referred to in the local press) had dragged the containers across the grass to a waiting lorry nearby. The police began an immediate search, but the thieves had made a quick getaway.

The following year, again under cover of the dark
winter night in Perthshire, the gang broke into the
bonded warehouse at the Aldour Distillery in Pitlochry.
On the night of 10th December 1931, the thieves
sawed through three quarter inch iron bars, on a
window of the store. Then, carefully removing the bars
so that they could be replaced, they quietly climbed
into the building. In a similar fashion the whisky was
syphoned into containers and carried through the
long grass to a waiting vehicle. Eighty gallons of whisky
were taken and, even though the police surmised that
the operation must have taken a long time, nobody
saw or heard anything. The bars on the window were
carefully replaced, so a cursory inspection would not
reveal any wrongdoing. The theft was discovered the
next day. Once again, the gang had got clean away.

A year later, almost to the day, the gang struck again.
This time their target was the Ballechin Distillery, near
Grandtully. The distillery was no longer operational,
but it was still used to store casks of whisky. On this
occasion the gang again cut through iron bars on
the windows to secure entry. Once inside they again
syphoned the whisky into containers and removed it
to a motor car and lorry parked just yards from the
Grandtully to Logierait road. This time, however, they
were careless. Their haul could have been far more
lucrative. They failed to notice a large number of casks
in a different part of the warehouse. Their vehicles
were parked in full sight of the road and, although it

was dark and late, a couple driving back to Aberfeldy noticed the car and lorry and even joked "I bet they're after the whisky!". Two further witnesses saw the vehicles heading toward Logierait and, although surprised to see them, failed to take down the registration numbers.

The theft was bold indeed. Mr McLean, the local Excise Officer, lived only 300 yards from the distillery and was soon on the scene. He also revealed that a previous attempt had been made on the distillery two months before but had been aborted.

The gang disappeared into the night again and despite a huge effort by the police, were never caught. Perhaps, on reading the reports in the newspaper, they realised how close they had come to being caught? Or perhaps their haul from the three robberies (worth more than £60,000 today) was enough?

Whatever the answer, whisky has provided a valuable income resource to the population of Highland Perthshire for the past 250 years, both legally and illegally.

# THE MANIAC
# OF BREADALBANE

In 1888 the entire country was gripped by the Whitechapel Murders in London. Would the killer strike again? Would he be caught? Just who was Jack the Ripper? Rural Scotland seemed a very long way from this gruesome story. However, one enterprising newspaper, *The Evening Telegraph*, sought to tap into our fascination for the macabre. One resourceful correspondent for the paper was reminded of a man who wandered the high roads of Perthshire 90 years previously, threatening women with a knife or razor blade. No records are now available from the original reporting of the assaults in the 1790s; however, we are fortunate to have this interesting recollection of the story from the pages of *The Dundee Evening Telegraph* (known locally as 'The Tele'), dated Friday 28th September 1888.

Reproduced below, the account uses both the language of its time, and of the 1790s. The piece offers a unique insight into the language, culture and social values of a time gone by:

## THE MANIAC OF BREADALBANE:
## A STORY OF NINETY YEARS AGO

In the month of October 1799 there died in the
Tolbooth of Perth a lunatic prisoner who was charged
with a series of offences similar to those which had
been perpetrated a few years earlier in the streets of
London, and also similar, in intention at least, to the
Whitechapel atrocities of our own day, which have
spread affright and horror over the metropolis.

Angus McDonald was his name, and he obviously
had come from the humblest parentage, but to what
parish he belonged was uncertain. He had attained the
age of manhood when he appeared in the county of
Breadalbane, as a homeless and friendless, half-witted
wanderer, nobody knowing anything about him, and
he being always evasive on the subject of his birthplace
and connections.

He roamed vaguely in the districts around Loch Tay,
doing any little 'orra jobs' [1]  as a common labourer,
and when out of work and under pressure of want,
seeking substance by begging – careless of where he
rested his head at nights, whether in barn or byre, or
beneath a brush of broom on the windy moor. Though
'silly', as was evident at a glance, he was quiet, good-
natured, easily pleased, and not infrequently jocose
when times were favourable. But eventually it was his
misfortune that "a change came o'er the spirit of his
dream" [2], when Cupid, on frolic intent, aimed a love-
arrow at his soft and facile heart.

"Daft folk" are by no means unsusceptible of the
tender passion; and Angus grew deeply enamoured
of a blooming young quean [3], a servant in one of
the farm-towns where he was hired during part of
the harvest season. Kirsty, out of sheer fun, having
encouraged his advances, her admirer resolved to
strike the iron while it was hot, and with little more
ado proposed in downright earnest that the twain
should get buckled at the next Martinmas term.[4]
She would then have her half year's "penny fee" to
add to her savings in the "neuk o' her kist" [5], and he
in the interval would work like a horse, at whatever
offered, and lay by in his spleuchan [6] every farthing
he earned, and they would get a cottar house [7] and a
cow and start in life! Kirsty listened to all this when it
was propounded behind a peat-stack in the dusk of
the lown gloaming [8], and blushingly whispered, with a
sly twinkle in her eye, what seemed like sweet consent.
Poor Angus was now the happiest of mortals. On
quitting the place he set himself vigorously to fulfil his
part of the bargain. The weeks sped swiftly by in the
"pleasures of hope"; but

"When the wan leaf from the birk tree was fa'lin',
And Martinmas dowie had wound up the year" [9]

Behold! To the utter amazement, the unbounded
wrath and despair, of the bridegroom expectant,
he learned how grossly he had been deceived, how
ruthlessly his prospects of future happiness were
shattered. The adorable but faithless Kirsty was
wedded and away with a cousin of her own – shipped

for America, where her two brothers were settled as farmers.

Whatever small modicum of reason Angus had hitherto possessed was fairly upset by this disappointment. More than that, the demon of revenge entered and swayed his lunatic brain. He had been foully wronged, and he would have his revenge. But on whom could he wreak it? Kirsty was out of his reach – the foamy billows of the Atlantic rolling between her and him. In his maddened cogitations he came to the conclusion that the whole fair sex together were false, and therefore to women in general he swore eternal enmity. The furies working in his head impelled him to attack any solitary female whom he chanced to meet in lone places by threatening and endeavouring to murder her! It does not appear that he ever inflicted wounds on his intended victims, as they either succeeded in beating him off, or escaped by speed of foot, or where rescued by somebody whom their outcries brought to their assistance. On the other hand, there was a cowardly cunning in his madness; for in his roving far and wide among the hills and glens he took special care to demean himself humbly and inoffensively at house doors where he sought work or begged bread; and he was never accused of theft, which showed that he could distinguish quite well betwixt meum and tuum [10]. So he went on, living as a waif of the wilds, and indulging in his homicidal propensity whenever he saw opportunity; and as he continually shifted about – scouring through the

heart of the Breadalbane highlands, picking up a
subsistence, none could scarcely tell how, it was far
from easy to get him under restraint in days when no
rural police existed. Here, then, was this madman
wandering at his own will, somewhat like a wolf or mad
dog, and nobody able to lay him by the heels.

When things come to the worst they mend, quoth
the proverb. The criminal authorities of the county
bestirred themselves, and with much difficulty Angus
was seized and brought down to the Perth Tolbooth,
a rough old prison overlooking the Tay at the foot of
the High Street. He was tried before the Sheriff, who
pronounced upon him the sentence of perpetual
banishment from the shire – a common mode in that
day of getting rid of troublesome and unruly vagrants.

For a season Angus traversed other parts of the
country without apparently giving offence; but he
sighed for his old haunts, and at length ventured to
show his face in the Breadalbane highlands, where
he soon resumed his former ferocious practice,
threatening women with death. In particular, he very
nearly sacrificed a poor woman's life in a wood near
Taymouth; and once more the beagles of the law were
on the quest for him. On 9th January 1799 Mr William
Ross, writer in Perth and Procurator Fiscal for the
County, presented a petition to the Sheriff, setting
forth the following statement of facts:-

"That a man named Angus McDonald, a good deal
deranged in the mind, has for some years past
travelled through Breadalbane, and has often put

women in fear by threatening to
take away their lives by cutting their
throats, and has actually made
several attempts.

About three or four weeks ago
he came up with a woman,
wife of a Duncan Dewar, in the
neighbourhood of Taymouth, on
the high road which goes through
a wood, pulled her down and took
out a small knife, sharpening it on
his shoe, put it up again, saying it would not do; then
took a razor out of a parcel, his knee all the while
keeping her down, and just as he was taking the razor
two men on horseback relieved the woman and horse-
whipped him.

That the said Angus McDonald was formerly
committed to prison for a similar charge, and in
consequence thereof was banished from the County
for life; but either from his perverse nature, or the
derangement of his mind, he still perseveres in his
improper conduct, and people are very much in
danger from him when he thinks he is master of
them; and it is absolutely necessary that he is again
secured to prevent fatal consequences from his future
conduct."

The Sheriff granted warrant to apprehend the said
Angus McDonald within the Tolbooth of Perth and
recommended the petitioner to find out the parish in
which Angus was born, or in which he had last resided

for three years altogether.

For a while after the issue of the warrant it became about as easy to apprehend Angus as to catch a bird by putting salt on its tail[11]. Day by day he was heard of, here, there, everywhere, but could be found nowhere. Heathery mountains, shaggy glens, deep corries, dark woods, "moors and moors, many, O", were all searched in vain, and it appeared that none but a Red Indian could have a chance of running him down on the trail. But at last the persistent pursuit was crowned with success. Angus was pounced upon by the myrmidoms[12] of justice, and consigned to his former cold quarters in Perth Tolbooth. There, before being brought to trial, he fell ill of a distemper[13], which speedily proved mortal - the petition against him being endorsed thus:

"Oct, 12 – Angus McDonald died"

And so Breadalbane was finally relieved of the pest of the homicidal woman-hater. It need scarce be added that the Fiscal's inquiries elicited no reliable information on the prisoner's parish of birth, etc."

1.  Orra – 17th century English word for odd. Now archaic.

2.  From Lord Byron's *The Dream*, written in 1816. An oft used quote during the 19th Century.

3.  Quean - An old word, used mainly in Scotland during the 18th and 19th Century, referring to a young, badly behaved girl, usually unmarried, perhaps a prostitute.

4.  Martinmas Term. Traditionally the 11th November, the term

date for the hiring and removal of servants and the time when unpaid accounts became due.

5.  "Neuk o' her Kist" - Neuk, meaning corner, or recess. Kist – was a servant's chest or trunk.

6.  Spleuchan – a pouch, used usually for money or tobacco.

7.  Cottar House. Scottish, or German, term for a peasant farmer's house.

8.  Lown gloaming – the peaceful and calm twilight.

9.  An excerpt from a traditional Scottish song, entitled *Lucy's Flittin'*. The subject matter of the song being an apt choice for this story. "Martinmas dowie" refers to the dull and dreary period following Martinmas.

10. Meum and Tuum. "Mine and yours". Latin term usually applied to someone who could distinguish between their own property and somebody else's

11. An old tale, usually told to children, in the false belief that it would be easier to catch a bird.

12. From Greek Mythology, the myrmidons were soldiers, or followers, who would carry out their orders ruthlessly and without question

13. Distemper, an infectious viral condition, often used in the 15th-19th century to describe an infectious and flu like virus with symptoms such as sweating.

# THE TOLLROAD KILLER

On the morning of 28th September 1867 Charles
McDonald, an itinerant traveller, banged on the door
of East Tomnagrew Farmhouse, along the Amulree
to Dunkeld toll road. Donald McDuff answered. He
was confronted with a shocking site. On his threshold
stood McDonald, a man of about 40, average height,
stout build and 'reckless' appearance. His dirty clothes
were torn and marked with blood. Both his hands
and face were also bloodstained. He appeared to be
limping and in pain. Most striking of all, however, was
a knife cut, across his throat, running from ear to ear.
Blood trickled down his neck and his collar, throat and
chest were noticeably discoloured.

When McDuff asked him what had happened,
McDonald said that he and his wife had been sleeping
alongside the toll road, when they been woken by
two men who had jumped over the hedgerow. The
two men, McDonald claimed, had beaten him nearly
senseless, then dragged his wife away. He feared that
they intended to rape her and tried to go to her
assistance. He had followed them east along the road
towards Dunkeld, he said, but the two men had turned

back and attacked him again, dragging him 200 yards along the road and throwing him over the parapet of the bridge in Trochry, into the river below. He feared that he had broken his back and exclaimed that he was lucky to be alive.

Charles McDonald insisted that someone go with him to view the bridge and look for his wife. Peter MacDougall, a ploughman at Tomnagrew Farm, accompanied him. In Trochry, at the bridge over the river, MacDonald pointed out a birch branch in the water, which had spots of blood on its leaves. It was at least a 60 feet drop to the water, with many sharp rocks protruding from the river, and steep, unforgiving banks.

Meanwhile, about 500 yards east of Tomnagrew a medical student, named John MacDonald, made the gruesome discovery of a woman's body, slumped beside the road. As he approached, he at first presumed that she was drunk. However, he soon realised it was far more serious. Her head had been smashed with a heavy blunt instrument and there was significant trauma to the face. Her breast-bone and several ribs were broken and her body bore several violent cuts and abrasions. There was also a distinct trail of blood, indicating that the victim had been dragged for at least 30 yards.

Her body was removed and placed in a locked room at Tomnagrew Farmhouse. The local Police Sergeant for the district, Robert McBean, was called. He, in turn, sent for Dr Murray from Dunkeld and the Procurator Fiscal for Perthshire, Mr Meville Jameson. Mr Jameson, who happened to be close by in Dunkeld, came immediately. His suspicions were aroused straight away. Such was the drop from the bridge, it would have been nearly impossible for a person to survive a fall from such a height. The blood on Charles McDonald's clothing, which he claimed as the result of the cut to his throat, did not seem to match the injury. He also had cuts and scratches on his forearms, consistent with those made by someone defending themselves against him. Dr Murray examined McDonald's throat, the wound proving to be very superficial. Its unusual "V" shape also indicated (to the experienced Doctor) that it had been self-inflicted. McDonald claimed that he did not own a knife as he did not smoke and therefore had no need to cut tobacco. He also seemed to be making a remarkable recovery from his broken back. In fact, Dr Murray could find no evidence of any injury to his body. Charles McDonald was immediately detained for questioning and a post mortem was ordered. The body was quickly identified as being that of Mrs McDonald. The doctor discovered at least sixteen injuries to the body, most of them penetrating to the bone. There was also extensive evidence of previous injuries to the scalp and many cuts and bruises on the arms and legs. It appeared that the breast bone had been broken by someone standing, or stamping, on the victim.

A search of the ground at the scene of the crime proved fruitful. A piece of birch tree, about two feet six inches in length and five inches wide, was discovered. It was covered in blood. Next to it was a heavy piece of sandstone, also heavily stained with blood. McDonald could offer no explanation when questioned, and remained tight lipped throughout his interrogation.

The Amulree to Dunkeld road was a far busier place in the Victorian era than it appears today. A popular coaching route, the toll road was lined with small hamlets and houses (mostly abandoned today), two inns and even a small brewery at Strathbraan. The road was frequented by labourers, ploughmen and merchants, making their way to work or to Dunkeld on a twice daily basis. Many vagrants camped in the fields alongside the road and, along with locals, drank in the inns before walking long distances home again.

The police found the task of finding witnesses a comparatively easy one. Susan Mellon, a widow from Glen Quaich, had been drinking in the inn at Deanshaugh and shared a drink with Charles

McDonald and his wife on the 27th September. Later that evening she joined them at their camp for a smoke. However, she left hastily after the family became violent in a drunken argument over money. Later, she passed an acquaintance who remarked that he "had seen the tinkers" and that "he was killing her". Susan Mellon, together with her daughter, decided to sleep the night in the cart shed at Tomnagrew and were awoken at one o'clock in the morning by the sound of arguing. They distinctly heard a woman cry out: "It's dune noo, you've dune it noo". The children of Charles McDonald spoke of his cruelty towards their mother, frequently pulling her by her hair, punching her and dropping stones on her whilst she slept.

Even more damning was the evidence of John Forbes, a shepherd, who had seen Mrs McDonald sprawled by the roadside, covered in blood. He shouted to Charles McDonald, who was crouched down nearby, to help her out of the road. McDonald replied that he was looking for a bottle of whisky and refused to help.

William Stewart, a weaver, had passed the McDonald's roadside camp earlier in the evening and clearly heard a couple arguing and the sickening sound of someone being punched. Robert MacNaughton, a ploughman, passed MacDonald on the toll road. MacDonald, in his drunken state, said to MacNaughton "would you like to see a murder?".

Perhaps the most poignant of all was the testimony of the Reverend Alexander Stewart, from The Manse at Amulree, who passed the woman on the side of the road at around 8pm. He clearly heard her call out to her daughter "Jenny, I've been murdered!". He also witnessed Charles McDonald disappear hastily into the trees, upon his approach.

With the weight of evidence now stacked against McDonald a trial date was set at the High Court of The Justiciary in Edinburgh, for Monday 16th December 1867. The Lord Justice Clerk, Lord Ardmillan, presided. Despite the weight of evidence Charles McDonald pled "Not Guilty" but could offer no defence in court. The sheer number of witnesses offered by the Lord Advocate, on behalf of the prosecution, coupled with McDonald's unlikely story of being thrown over a bridge, convinced the jury of his guilt in the crime of murder. By a majority verdict, the jury requested that the death penalty not be applied, as they could find no evidence of "premeditation or malice aforethought".

The Lord Justice, however, proclaimed that the seriousness of the crime allowed for no other sentence than one of death by hanging. He added that the appeal for leniency would be forwarded to the Court of Appeal, and that McDonald should make his peace with God. The sentence was read to the Court and the date of the execution was set for 8th January 1868, at Perth Prison, between the hours of 8am and 10am.

In a final twist to the story, exactly one week later, the Home Office granted Charles McDonald a stay of execution. At "the mercy of the Crown", his sentence of death was commuted to life imprisonment for the crime. The message was relayed immediately to the Lord Provost of Perth, and McDonald would serve out the rest of his sentence at Her Majesty's pleasure, behind the high walls of Perth Prison.

# ON A WING
# AND A PRAYER

During the autumn of 1877, Gavin Campbell The Marquess Of Breadalbane, was at the height of his wealth and popularity in Aberfeldy and the surrounding area. He had succeeded to the title in 1871, following the death of his father. Still only 26, he had recently married Lady Alma Graham, owned the impressive Breadalbane estates and could count members of the Royal Family and the Government amongst his friends.

As a young man he had lived at Moness House, overlooking Aberfeldy, but following the death of his father he moved to Taymouth Castle at Kenmore. The Marquess decided that he required a private chaplain for his estate and advertised for the position in the society papers and journals. The stipend was generous and included the letting of Moness House as spacious and luxurious accommodation. Not surprisingly, the advertisement attracted lots of interest. Among the applicants was the Reverend William Bentley. 'Every inch the gentleman', Bentley was charming, engaging,

with a respectable wife, and new born son. The
Marquess Of Breadalbane engaged Bentley, who took
up residence at Moness House in January 1878. The
Marquess even persuaded the new tenant of Moness
House, Dr Reid, to sub-let the substantial property to
Bentley, on attractive rental terms

The Reverend Bentley was immediately welcomed into
the community, and soon found himself an honoured
guest at social functions and dinner parties. He was
a familiar sight at shoots, cricket matches, curling
competitions and gatherings around the town. Always
well dressed and gentlemanly in his conduct, he
enjoyed the respect that came with his position in the
Breadalbane social circle.

Bentley opened credit accounts with the local
merchants and shopkeepers. Butchers, grocers, bakers,
milliners and wine merchants. With such an esteemed
position he also obtained 'easy terms' with the town's
tailors, shoemakers and even the Highland Railway
Company. Any doubts expressed by the shopkeepers

as to his creditworthiness were quickly dispelled by a friendly reminder of the nobility of his employer and of his higher calling.

He even ordered a fully sprung wagonette from WM Thomson Coachbuilders in Perth. The carriage, with side facing passenger seats, left and right, front facing driver's seat and complete with fittings, was to be delivered to Moness House upon completion, and paid for in three yearly instalments.

As spring became summer the shopkeepers of Aberfeldy began to express concern at the non-payment of their accounts. The Reverend assured everyone that reimbursement would be made very soon. Any doubts, or expressions of concern, were deflected by a reminder of his noble employer. Bentley's expensive tastes did not seem to match his income.

Perhaps there was another way he could supplement his salary and continue his lavish lifestyle?

During the summer the Rev. Bentley inserted the following advertisement in *The Times* and in the London sporting papers:

*A DELIGHTFUL HOUSE IN THE HIGHLANDS AND PRIVATE TUITION*

*Pupils prepared for the Army, Navy, Church, etc.*
*- A Nobleman's Chaplain offers the above.*
*Most healthy climate, magnificent scenery, fishing, shooting, riding, boating, cricket, refined domestic comfort, and*

*desirable companionship. Address, Moness House, Aberfeldy,*
*Rev WM Bentley.*

This was followed by an even more superlative advertisement in *The Field* magazine, which described Aberfeldy as "The Mentone Of Scotland". Mentone is a beautiful medieval town on the French Riveria, well known for its warm climate, beaches and attractive gardens. The artistic licence appeared to be successful and soon Bentley welcomed his first guest, a young gentleman from London who brought his hunting dog with him, expecting to enjoy the hunting opportunities that were advertised. He was quickly followed by a young lady, hoping to enjoy the desirable companionship at the Highland retreat. Soon Moness House had welcomed six tenants, all hoping to enjoy the benefits of a desirable Highland existence, and all paying a substantial rent. The Reverend William Bentley, within a year of arriving in Aberfeldy, had supplemented his income to the tune of £1,200 per annum (more than £140,000 today). He had yet to pay a bill, including his rent.

Time appeared to be running out for the mendacious minister. One by one his tenants had left. None of the activities he had promised were delivered. The very first guest to arrive soon found out that the only hunting available for his dog was rat baiting in the yard. Bentley's income suffered, yet he attempted to maintain his lifestyle. His bills remained unpaid.

By Martinmas (11th November), the traditional
point in the calendar that accounts were settled,
the merchants and shopkeepers of Aberfeldy were
extremely worried. Despite many promises, their
accounts remained unpaid. 15 traders were owed
payment. In addition, Dr Reid was due substantial
sums in rent and WM Coachbuilders had not yet been
paid for their custom-built carriage. Two creditors
alone were owed £560 (£65,000 today). An emergency
meeting of creditors was held in the town on the
evening of Monday 13th January 1879, to decide on
a course of action. They had received a letter from
the Reverend Bentley's wife, explaining that he was
seriously ill with a fever, and unable to attend to his
business. She pleaded for more time to pay, assuring
the merchants that her husband would bring all his
outstanding accounts up to date.

However, at the exact moment that the meeting
was taking place, the Reverend William Bentley had
packed a bag and, turning his collar to the snow and
cold, was making his way to Ballinluig Station. He had
chosen the precise moment of the meeting, knowing
all his creditors would be gathered in one place, to slip
away from Aberfeldy under cover of darkness. Rather
than take a train from Aberfeldy Station, and invite
suspicion, Bentley chose to trudge the 10 miles to
Ballinluig Station on a dark, cold and snowy evening.

Once his disappearance was realised, enquiries were
hastily made. It appeared that he had taken a train
from Ballinluig and headed south to England. Bentley

absconded from Aberfeldy on that night, leaving debts to his creditors totalling £1,200 (£140,000 today).

He was never seen again.

Almost a year later, with no sign of the Reverend, the fallout continued in the courts. WM Thomson Coachbuilders of Perth desired the return of their purpose-built wagonette, arguing that as payment was never received, ownership had never passed to Rev Bentley. Dr Reid claimed that – as the carriage was still stored at Moness House – it should be sold to realise debts due to him. Perth Sheriff's Court found in favour of Dr Reid and WM Thomson were left with an unpaid debt and additional court costs. It was also remarked in court that the likelihood of any of Bentley's creditors receiving adequate recompense was extremely remote.

Interestingly, Dr Reid was represented in court by Charles Forbes, from Aberfeldy. In one of the many strange coincidences that mark the stories covered in this book, Forbes would later be involved in another sensational case that would rock the Highland Perthshire community (covered in the chapter *Last Seen at Killin*)

For the unfortunate traders of Aberfeldy, that was the last they would ever see, or hear, of the Reverend William M Bentley. It was an expensive lesson in trust, which many could not afford to repeat.

With the benefit of modern research techniques, however, we can add a little to the story of just what did become of the missing minister. It is thought that Bentley originated from Yorkshire, however he may well have arrived in Aberfeldy from elsewhere. Presumably he provided The Marquess Of Breadalbane with suitable references. However, it was common in the Victorian era for these to be forged. Appointments were often made on trust, based on the applicants (perceived) social position.

It appears, following his hasty departure from Aberfeldy, Bentley headed for the southwest of England. Presumably happy to put some distance between himself and Scotland. The next we hear of the Rev Bentley is in 1893. Bentley and his family were renting a house just outside Bath and, although he referred to himself around town as the "Rev William Bentley", there is no evidence he was actually employed by the church. Instead, it seems, he was using a familiar subterfuge to supplement his income. He had advertised for tenants, offering to teach them the art of farming, for a fee of £50. A gentleman called Mr Hogg had sent his son to Bentley's home, in the hope that the young man could learn the trade. However, it became patently obvious that Bentley was not offering any tuition at all. Mr Hogg made further enquires and found Bentley to be "without means or principle". He immediately contacted Prescott & Co, his bank in Bath, and put a stop on the first cheque of £20 that he had written to Bentley.

Bentley, however, altered the name on the cheque and presented it at Colmer & Company, Drapers, in Bath.

The cheque was used to purchase goods to the value of £7 and change was given to Bentley. Judgement was given in favour of the plaintiff, and the action seems to have been enough to drive Bentley from the town.

Within two years though, Bentley obtained a legitimate ecclesiastical appointment as the Rector of St Mary's, at Honeychurch in Devon and as the Vicar of nearby Brushford. The joint appointment brought with it a combined salary of £78 (approximately £10,000 today). It seems though, that by 1899 Bentley was blighted by money troubles again. A local building company, Paynes & Son, obtained a court judgement against Bentley for £34 19s 7d, for unpaid bills, relating to work undertaken at the Rectory Cottage. In 1901 a further application was made at Okehampton Court for judgement against Bentley, by a Mr Dunn. However, it appeared that Bentley was already paying £5 per month in other outstanding judgements, and had no spare income to realistically repay any further debts. He was already receiving an allowance from a charitable fund for poor clergymen (The Victoria Fund) and appeared a much more sympathetic defendant in court.

By 1901 it seems Bentley was paying for, at least, some of his previous over spending. Running away was no longer the easy option it had been in Aberfeldy, 22 years earlier. Bentley was a much older man, with no private means and, as he explained to the court, had a wife and five children, one of whom was an invalid.

No further mention of the Reverend William Bentley seems to exist, so it may be assumed he lived out the rest of his life in relative obscurity and poverty.

# THE VICTIM
# NAMES HIS KILLER

At half past five on the early morning of 9th April
1889, Duncan Reid (a 26-year-old farm foreman at
Tullypowrie Farm, situated on the north side of the
River Tay, close to the Tullypowrie Burn, about a mile
from Grandtully Station) walked from the dwelling
house at the farm to the steadings. As he walked past
the barn, he noticed his master, Duncan Robertson,
slumped in front of the barn door. Robertson was lying
on his left side, his head resting on a circular stone.
The upper, stable style, doors were open, the bottom
ones closed, as if Robertson had just passed through
them. As Reid approached him, he noticed that blood
covered his forehead and one side of his face. Duncan
Reid saw no one else in the courtyard, although it was
not yet fully daylight.

Reid enquired in Gaelic: "What is the matter?"

"Oh that John, oh that John," came the answer.

He tried to help Duncan Robertson to his feet.
Robertson was a large, strongly built and fit man of
58, but was unable to stand. Reid rested Robertson's

head down and looked inside the barn. In the corner, amongst the piles of hay, was the figure of John Taylor. Just rising, Taylor was hurriedly dressing. An itinerant worker who moved between different farms in the region, working for a few days, and usually sleeping in barns or outbuildings, Taylor was known as "Jocky the tramp". Duncan Reid asked Taylor to help carry Duncan Robertson into the barn. They did so, and laid Robertson on a bed of straw. Reid indicated that he was going to fetch help. Before doing so, he enquired: "What has come over Mr Robertson?". Taylor, however, did not answer. Reid ran to the farmhouse and met Mrs Margaret McLagan. Aged 68, she was Duncan Robertson's widowed elder sister. She explained that Robertson had left the house at 5am, intending to wake Taylor, in order that they could feed the cattle.

Entering the barn, Mrs McLagan also asked Taylor if he knew what had happened to her brother. Taylor again remained silent. She challenged him, which seemed to anger Taylor. She knew that her brother frequently had great trouble in waking Taylor, whose temper was greatly aroused if woken from his slumber. The group's first priority, however, was to move Duncan Robertson into the farmhouse. The farmer was finding speech difficult, his face was covered in blood and his sister noticed a large puncture wound in his forehead, just above his right eye. Taylor was told to wait in the barn, while the Police and doctor were sent for.

Upon their arrival, a search was carried out in the barn. On the floor, behind the doors was found a pitchfork, damaged and showing traces of blood. The lower stable style doors, which were closed when Reid had found Duncan Robertson slumped outside earlier in the morning, were now open. Taylor was asked why the doors were closed when Robertson was first discovered. Taylor responded that Robertson must have pulled them to as he left. The police doubted this, knowing the weak and injured condition Robertson was found in. Taylor was again challenged and finally admitted that he had quarrelled with Duncan Robertson. He was immediately arrested and taken to Perth. Due to the perilous condition of Duncan Robertson, the authorities in Perth made the unusual move of sending Sheriff Grahame and Mr Melville Jameson (the depute Procurator Fiscal) directly to Tullypowrie Farm to take a deposition from the farmer. On the Sheriff's arrival, later in the afternoon of the same day, he was hastily shown up to Robertson's bedroom. The farmer, unfortunately, was having great difficulty in constructing sentences and no worthwhile statement could be taken. However, two days later, on 11th April 1889, Robertson seemed slightly better, and able to speak in short sentences, so Sheriff Grahame was again summoned to Tullypowrie.

Lucid and concise, Robertson was able to explain the full circumstances of the events that had taken place two days earlier. He had awoken and gone to the barn at 5am, to wake Taylor for work. Taylor had refused to get up and help. Frustrated, Robertson had pulled at Taylor's sleeve, attempting to shake him from his stupor. Angrily, Taylor threatened to strike him with a pitchfork. Seeing Taylor picking up the pitchfork, Robertson turned to leave the barn. As he did so, Taylor struck him in the small of the back. Surprised, he turned around. At that moment Taylor thrust the pitchfork into Robertson's forehead. One of the prongs entered the orbital plate of the frontal bone, just above the right eye, with such force, that the eyeball was dislodged. The prong of the pitchfork passed through the bone and cavity, entering the brain matter. Robertson slumped outside the door of the barn. Taylor then closed the lower half of the doors and proceeded to dress.

On Friday 17th April, eight days after the attack, Robertson passed away. A post-mortem was ordered and took place at Tullypowrie the following day. Dr Stirling, from Perth, and Dr Haggart, from Aberfeldy, carried out the examination. A record of part of their report still exists:

*We are of the opinion (1) that death was caused by haemorrhage into the brain and extensive destruction of brain substance; (2) this haemorrhage was produced by direct injury to the blood vessels and the substance of the brain; (3) that the injury was caused by violence; (4) that the violence was from without, and caused by some sharp instrument thrust into the cavity of the orbit through the orbital plate of the frontal bone, and into the substance of the brain itself.*

Taylor was charged with murder, at an initial hearing in Perth, but pled "Not Guilty". The accused stated: "he was pulling me out of bed, and the row started."

A trial date was set for 27th June 1889. Taylor's counsel, Mr John A Stewart, claimed a special defence, under the terms of the Criminal Procedure Act. He informed the court that he intended to argue that a "quarrelsome disposition" on the part of Duncan Robertson led to the row and the attack. After some consultation Lord Shand dismissed the argument, stating that it was not valid as form of "special defence". John Taylor, who had already pled "Not Guilty", was advised to plead guilty to a charge of culpable homicide.

John Taylor seemed to garner much sympathy from Lord Shand, and from those present in the Perth Courthouse. Before passing away, Duncan Robertson expressed no ill will towards John Taylor. There had been no premeditation and it could not be proved that Taylor had intended to kill Robertson with the brutal attack. "Jocky the tramp" cut a sympathetic figure in court. He could not read or write and possessed no previous criminal record.

Lord Shand, whilst noting the serious and violent nature of the attack, found Taylor not guilty of murder, but guilty of culpable homicide. By today's standards the sentence of 12 months imprisonment seems incredibly light for such a serious assault, however entirely in keeping with the times. Other crimes, which today might be treated with far more understanding, were taken far more seriously. For example, the death of a baby in childbirth, where the pregnancy had been concealed from the family, would routinely be met with a charge of child murder.

Tullypowrie passed into the hands of Duncan Robertson's younger brother John. Aged 52, John was also a farmer and took over the establishment, to run alongside his own, nearby farm.

John Taylor served his 12 months imprisonment, perhaps rueing his inability to wake early for work, and was released in 1890. Perhaps he returned to his vagrant lifestyle, however he did not reappear in the Strathtay area again. Probably preferring to keep his distance. He did surface in the Dunfermline area, however, being fined 40 shillings and sentenced to 30 days imprisonment, for an assault on a railway worker in 1896. The railway engineer had disturbed Taylor, who was sleeping rough in the sidings at the time. Old habits, it appears, never die!

# FOOTPRINTS
# IN THE SNOW

There are many common threads throughout the
stories that weave this book together. Tragedy, temper,
desperation, greed and even mystery. This tale,
however, contains two key factors – which, sadly, often
go together - drunkenness and stupidity.

In the early hours of 20th December 1938, a family
living alongside Haggart's Woollen Mill in Taybridge
Terrace, Aberfeldy, were awoken by a flickering light
shining through the bedroom window and reflecting
on the wall of the room. On rising from their beds
and opening the curtains, they looked across to
the woollen mill. Clearly visible from the seven
symmetrical windows on the ground and first floor of
the stone structure, was the unmistakable glow of fire.
The police were sent for immediately. On arrival they
discovered a broken window on the ground floor, from
where it appeared entry had been affected. On the sill,
and on the snow on the ground nearby, were several
drops of blood, where presumably the intruder had
injured himself whilst forcing his way into the mill.

Once inside the police constables discovered two separate fires, one on the ground floor and one on the first floor. Both had taken some time and trouble to start. A pile of books, oily rags, rolls of cloth and flammable machine grease had been gathered, from different points in the mill, and placed in two heaps. Each mound had then been set alight and left to burn. The officers were able to put both fires out with extinguishers, which were located liberally about the premises. Fortunately, the flammable nature of the materials stored in the mill had meant the fire precaution measures at the mill were excellent. Despite severe damage having been caused to the mill, the immediate danger was averted. Next the police communicated with all the local stations and every patrol car was despatched to search the area. The Pitlochry patrol car, making its way carefully along the Strathtay Road in the freshly fallen snow, noticed some fresh footprints, which appeared to lead away from the woollen mill. On reaching the mill they were able to clearly see the footprints leading up to the broken window, the drops of blood, and the footprints leading away from the scene of the crime. They decided to follow the prints, which did not require any special tracking skills. Their task made easy by the fresh snow, the occasional drop of blood (clearly visible against the crisp, clean fall), and the lack of any other prints at such a late hour. The constable tracked the footprints for several miles, back along the winding Strathtay Road, right up to the doorstep of a worker's cottage on the Balnasuim Estate in Strathtay. They entered the house and found its occupant, John Robertson, in bed. On examining Robertson and his bedroom, the officers found blood on his hand from a cut, and several items that had been stolen from the mill, in the room.

In what can only be called, an 'open and shut' case, John Robertson was sent to trial at Perth Sheriff's Court on 17th January 1939. Mr ML Howman, the Procurator Fiscal, described the events of the evening. Robertson admitted stealing several items and to "having culpably and recklessly set fire to the mill".

Speaking in Robertson's defence, Mr G Sharp explained that Robertson had been drinking in Aberfeldy during the evening of the 19th December. He had missed the last bus home and lost his way home in the dark. After breaking into the mill, he admitted stealing certain items but could not remember starting the fire. He claimed to be a trusted estate worker, earning 38 shillings a week.

Any hopes of sympathy, however, were short lived. Sheriff Valentine described the crime as a serious one. The employment opportunities of the mill workers had been put in jeopardy, damage of several hundred pounds had been caused (more than £30,000 today), and the excuse of not remembering starting the fire did little to help Robertson's cause.

John Robertson was sentenced to six months imprisonment, with Sheriff Valentine telling the court: "A man who behaved in that way, whether he was under the influence or not, was a criminal".

# FRANCIS METCALFE:
# ROBIN HOOD OR CONMAN?

The story of Francis William Metcalfe is one of war, adventure, prison, embezzlement, fraud, and an international manhunt. Polite, popular, clever and devious. Just how did this quietly spoken, considerate and sociable estate manager bring national attention to Aberfeldy and spark an international manhunt?

Francis Willey, a wealthy wool merchant from Bradford, who had recently been awarded the title Baron (or Lord) Barnby, purchased the Castle Menzies Estate, near Aberfeldy, following the death of Sir Neil Menzies. Later, he also acquired the adjoining Killiechassie estate, bringing him land totalling 17,000 acres. Lord Barnby's family home was the Blyth Estate in Nottinghamshire. Together with his business interests in Yorkshire, London and overseas in America, Lord Barnby employed more than 15,000 people worldwide.

Lord Barnby

He intended to leave the running of the Castle Menzies Estate to an estate manager and factor and advertised accordingly. In the spring of 1924 Francis Metcalfe, having read the advertisement, wrote to Lord Barnby at his Blyth Estate. No doubt impressed by Metcalfe's varied résumé, Barnby wired him, and Metcalfe duly travelled to Nottinghamshire for an interview.

Francis Metcalfe was born in Aberdeen on 9th April 1893 and educated at Aberdeen Grammar School, then at Aberdeen University, although records show he did not complete his education there. A small man, only 5 feet 2 inches in height, he had dark hair and spoke with

Francis Metcalfe

an Aberdonian accent. After beginning work at the Cawdor Estate Office, he worked in various factoring and farming posts until he enlisted in 1915 in the South Lancashire Regiment, aged 22. In November 1915 he was given a commission as a Second-Lieutenant and served in France and in the near arctic regions of Russia, as part of the North Russia Expeditionary Force (during which time he became a friend and confidant of Ernest Shackleton). In France he suffered, along with others in his platoon, the effects of mustard gas inhalation. Whilst posted in Russia he also caught pneumonia. His name was mentioned in despatches and he was promoted to Captain in October 1918.

After his demobilisation from the army in 1919,

Metcalfe received a payment of £400 (in gratuities and accumulated pay) and a disability pension of £52 (approximately £2,500 today), reducing to £26 for the next two years. He next obtained employment as a factor on an estate in County Galway, Ireland, at a salary of £300 per annum. However, his time on the estate, during the early 1920s, coincided with the Irish uprising and he was frequently accosted by members of Sinn Féin. The encounters were frightening, he was shot at on two occasions, then virtually chased from Irish shores.

Metcalfe, always referring to himself as Captain Metcalfe, claimed to have several well-paid positions, including one in London at a salary of £500, as well as being a partner in two other businesses. However, in September 1923, at Peterborough Court, he pleaded guilty to a charge of "obtaining money by false pretences" and received a six-month prison sentence.

We can safely assume that Metcalfe failed to mention the conviction in his discussions with Lord Barnby who, even at the age of 83, was a wise and experienced businessman.

Metcalfe and Lord Barnby met in June 1924. On his way to the appointment, Metcalfe first called in at the public library and looked up Lord Barnby in Burke's Peerage and Who's Who.

Lord Barnby told Metcalfe that he wanted a new factor for his Castle Menzies Estate, near Aberfeldy in Perthshire. He only spent a small proportion of the year there, he told Metcalfe, usually just for the shooting season. Lord Barnby explained that the former factor had caused friction between himself, the tenants and the employees, so he had decided to dismiss him.

"Would you be interested in the position?" Lord Barnby asked, "I would prefer a married man, because I wish the factor to take an interest in the district, and a wife would also be of assistance among the tenants."

"For the position you want me to occupy", replied Metcalfe, "£500 is a suitable figure."

"That is in excess of what I am prepared to pay" came the reply. "£250 is all I am prepared to pay."

"That is hopelessly inadequate", Metcalfe responded.

A long discussion followed. Metcalfe told Lord Barnby that he had already been offered a situation in Glasgow for £300, plus commission and travelling expenses. However, the position at Castle Menzies suited him better and he would accept it for £250 per annum, on the understanding that his remuneration would be increased to £450, after a three-month period, if Lord Barnby was happy with his work.

An agreement was reached, and Metcalfe commenced his employment in July 1924. He was given an estate cottage as part of his salary.

Metcalfe discovered, on his arrival, that Mr Dickson (the previous factor) had sent the business books and accounts to the auditors, meaning Metcalfe had no point of reference and no ledgers in which to keep record of accounts, bills, wages and other incomings and outgoings from the estate. He purchased a bundle of foolscap paper, ink and pens, and began to record the business of the estate.

He endeavoured to respect Lord Barnby's wishes and became a member of the local school's management board, Rotarian, also putting his name forward for the Parish Council. In the meantime, he engaged an assistant and began the work of paying wages, invoices, accounts and arranging trading agreements with local farmers and wholesalers. He was authorised to write small cheques (Lord and Lady Barnby had left a small quantity of blank signed cheques with him). For all other payments due, including wages to the 36 employees, his instructions were to telephone or write to Lord Barnby for funds.

So, with a system in place, the smooth running of the Castle Menzies Estate was assured. Or was it?

Metcalfe immediately discovered, however, that the current method of bookkeeping at the estate was not adequate and suggested a change to Lord Barnby.

From the very beginning Metcalfe had trouble in obtaining money to cover the outstanding accounts from Lord Barnby. The Postmaster contacted Metcalfe, soon after he began work. No payment had been received from Lord Barnby, he informed Metcalfe that the telephone line to the Castle Menzies Estate was about to be cut off due to non-payment of the account.

Metcalfe begged the Post Office not to cut off the service and promised to pay the bill from his own bank account. After having done so, he contacted Lord Barnby and requested that the money for the bill be paid back to him.

Metcalfe wrote to Lord Barnby on four occasions and requested that he send enough funds to cover the Estate's wage bill. After no reply was received, Metcalfe was forced to pay the wages from his own account. This happened on two further occasions. Metcalfe was forced to visit the bank in Aberfeldy and make a special arrangement with Mr Gardiner, the banks accountant, to arrange an overdraft. On the 20th February 1925, Metcalfe met again with Mr Gardiner of the Commercial Bank in Aberfeldy. He agreed to allow Metcalfe to write a cheque for £449 11s 8d (approximately £27,000 today) to cover the Estate's wage bill. Metcalfe showed Mr Gardiner the wages book and persuaded him to allow the cheque to be cashed. On contacting Lord Barnby, Metcalfe was told that Lord Barnby had been away on holiday.

Not a week passed without Metcalfe being forced to attempt contact with Lord Barnby, at his Blyth Estate. Sometimes he was successful in obtaining funds, to cover the Estate's accounts, on other occasions he was not. Payments were slow and only received after several attempts at contact.

It seems Metcalfe was not the only one to suffer in this way. Lady Barnby herself came to Metcalfe one day complaining that Fisher's Laundry in Aberfeldy would not deliver the Estate's supply of linen, as the account, totalling £60, had not been settled for a year.

Other accounts with local merchants, and a substantial monthly account with the Highland Railway Company were all in arrears and Metcalfe was forced to settle these from his own account too. He had, on occasion, to visit Perth Cattle Mart and various farms in the county, on Estate business, and had to pay his own expenses. He also frequently paid the expenses of other Estate employees.

During January 1925 Metcalfe paid £34 5s to the Motor Taxation Department of Perth County Council, to register a Morris Cowley Bullnose motor car belonging to Lord Barnby, in his own name. In February he purchased a gun for £12 10s, from PD Malloch's Gunsmiths.

Over the course of 12 months in the employment of Lord Barnby, Metcalfe claimed to have only received one month's salary.

The business books were clearly being incorrectly managed. The fact that Metcalfe paid suppliers and employees from his own account, then claimed payment back from Lord Barnby, was complicated. Metcalfe's use of blank, signed cheques from Lord Barnby was a system fraught with the potential for abuse. For example, if he needed access to cash, a cheque would be cashed. Metcalfe claimed later, that as there was no safe in the Estate Office, he would put the money into his own account "for safe keeping". Similarly, if whisky was required (for visitors, ploughing matches, social occasions, etc) he had been required to purchase this. Metcalfe felt it only right that he should be able to claim this expense back. Lord Barnby (it was later claimed in court) was the most unpopular landlord in the area. There was some friction in the area regarding his non-payment of the parish rates for Weem, his subscription to the Weem Ploughing Association, and a strike by Estate staff over the non-payment of wages.

Matters, it seems, were destined to come to a head.

In May 1925, the Inland Revenue announced an Income Tax audit on Lord Barnby's Castle Menzies business affairs. However, it was from this point onwards that Francis Metcalfe's behaviour became very odd, and certainly not that of an innocent, and wronged, man. In June 1925 he visited Mr Edwards, the shipping agent, in Perth and enquired about a passport. He told the shipping agent that he intended to take a holiday on the continent with friends. Metcalfe was duly issued with the new blue passport, introduced in 1921, containing 32 pages and signed by the Foreign Secretary. It entitled Metcalfe to travel to France, The Netherlands, Belgium, Spain and Portugal. He, in fact, did not go on the holiday he mentioned, instead choosing to remain at Castle Menzies.

On July 17th, the day of the visit to the Estate by the Inland Revenue auditors, Metcalfe announced that he was leaving to visit Macdonald, Fraser & Co in Perth, in connection with the purchase of farm machinery. He left early, prior to the arrival of the auditors, taking his Morris Cowley Bullnose car. Inside his suitcase were some of the Estate's papers, £80 in cash, the keys to a box (in which the remaining accounts were kept), and his passport.

Metcalfe filled the motor car with petrol in Aberfeldy at 8am and headed south to Perth. Once in the 'Fair City' Metcalfe was able to persuade the manager at MacDonald, Fraser & Co to cash him a cheque for £50 (originally made payable to Metcalfe, from Lord Barnby) and present him with £50 in notes. Metcalfe had crossed the cheque, making it payable to the company. This practice, in this era of instant bank transfers and internet banking, seems unusual – and susceptible to fraud. However, it was common practice in the 19th and early 20th century. A system of trust existed and, therefore, penalties were harsh for knowingly crossing and representing a stopped cheque. Unfortunately for Metcalfe, on presenting the cheque at their bank in Perth, McDonald, Fraser & Co discovered that Lord Barnby had previously stopped the cheque, and they were consequently £50 (£3,000 today) out of pocket. The police and Lord Barnby were contacted immediately and informed.

Meanwhile, Metcalfe had wasted little time in leaving Perth. By mid-afternoon he was in Stirling. He stopped at the Station Hotel in the city for refreshment, persuading the manager to store the Morris Cowley motor car there for him. Metcalfe told the hotel's manager he would contact him, as soon as he needed to, with instructions regarding the car. Metcalfe then boarded a train from Stirling to Glasgow. He was next seen in Glasgow, during the early evening, having supper with a 'stylishly dressed lady' at a Glasgow hotel. Metcalfe then boarded the late London, Midland & Scottish mail train for London. The following day he boarded the 2pm boat train at Victoria Station (having first changed £15 into French francs), reaching Dover in time to catch the 4.20pm sailing for Boulogne.

In the interim, the Perth County Constabulary had begun their enquiries. Lord Barnby was contacted and he immediately offered a £50 reward for information leading to the arrest of Francis Metcalfe. The audit at Castle Menzies revealed sums and payments to Metcalfe totalling more than £900 (£59,000 today), which were unaccounted for. A warrant was issued for Metcalfe's arrest on a charge of "embezzlement of the sum of £974 18s, from the Castle Menzies Estate belonging to Lord Barnby". It can be safely assumed that Lord Barnby's influence must have been substantial, since the response to Metcalfe's flight from justice was swift, considerable and wide ranging. Metcalfe's description was issued and wired to all Scottish police stations and Scotland Yard. It was presumed (due to Metcalfe's previous employment in County Galway) that he may well have travelled to Ireland, so a watch was placed on all west coast ports in Scotland. Officers were despatched to various departure points and a photograph of Metcalfe was circulated. In another extraordinary measure, considering the relatively minor nature of the offence, a description of Metcalfe was issued to the BBC for broadcast on the pioneering, new local radio network. At that time, due to technical limitations, a national, simultaneous broadcast was not possible.

When the police discovered that Metcalfe had applied for a passport, and that the passport was not among his belongings left at Castle Menzies, the search was widened. A description, and details of the warrant, were wired to the police in Paris, Amsterdam, Madrid, Lisbon and Brussels. Probably for the only time in Aberfeldy's history, an international police manhunt was underway for one of its residents.

Metcalfe spoke fluent French, which was not widely known, and had some acquaintances in France he had met during the war. After visiting Bethune, Avignon, Abbeville and Marseilles, he naturally gravitated towards Paris. Once in the French capital, using what money he had taken, plus the £50 downpayment he had received from the sale of the Morris Cowley, he rented a room in a small hotel opposite the Gare du Nord railway station. Here he passed his time drinking in the bistros and cafés, with his associates, strolling along the wide boulevards of the city, eating as cheaply as he could, and keeping notes of his experiences.

His description had been wired to the police on the continent, including to The Direction Régionale de Police Judiciaire de Paris (the headquarters of the

Paris police service) at 36 quai des Orfèvres. His details were then circulated to the various, smaller police stations in the 20 arrondissements that make up that vast and sprawling city.

Perhaps that might have been an end to the matter, had Metcalfe not made one crucial mistake. The overstretched Paris police had very little chance of locating one, indistinctive itinerant among the thousands who flocked to Paris during the 1920s. Their days were filled with a litany of petty theft, assaults, drunkeness and vagrancy, with which to deal.

With no clue as to Metcalfe's location, no paper trail and no reason to make the case a priority, the French police may never have traced his location. For Francis Metcalfe, however, his dwindling funds were becoming an increasing worry.

After eight weeks, he could wait no longer. Metcalfe telegraphed James Alexander Smith (the manager of the Station Hotel, in Stirling), at which he had left the Morris Cowley Bullnose motor car. Metcalfe offered to complete the sale of the motor car for a further £50. It seemed a good price for a relatively new, and hardly used model, and Smith agreed readily. Payment was to be made in two instalments of £25. The first payment was sent to Paris and Metcalfe sent the vehicle's log book by return. The recent Roads Act 1920 had enforced the registering of vehicles and the addition of a keeper's name to the documentation.

Mr Smith, from the Stirling Hotel, continued to use

the car for the next month, until it was spotted in Station Road, outside the hotel, by Sergeant John Cowie of the Stirling police. Mr Smith admitted to the police that he had purchased the car from Metcalfe, and was able to show the police Metcalfe's correspondence from Paris, detailing his address in the French capital. Following this revelation the police quickly contacted their counterparts in Paris.

Francis Metcalfe would later describe the events that followed :

*On the morning of 9th October (1925), I was sleeping peacefully in my bed in a little hotel near one of the chief railway stations in Paris, when I was rudely awakened by loud voices outside my door, accompanied by loud knocking thereon.*

*On opening, to inquire into the disturbance, I was greeted by two men in civil clothes, both pointing revolvers at my head, who informed me they were 'agents of the Police', and held a warrant for my arrest. I was questioned as to my identity, searched, and shown the warrant, which was in French.*

Metcalfe was taken to the Ministry of the Interior, details of the warrant and his identity were confirmed and he was transferred to prison to await his extradition to Scotland.

After a period of several weeks arrangements for Metcalfe's extradition were completed. During the complicated process he was locked away, enduring tough and unpleasant conditions, in a French prison. This incarceration was to gain Metcalfe much sympathy at his later trial.

Eventually, on 21st November, Deputy-Chief Constable John MacPherson made the long trip to France to collect Metcalfe and return him to Perth Prison, where he would await his trial. His application for bail was refused, the Sheriff citing Metcalfe as a considerable flight risk.

The trial date was set for 1st March 1926. It was to be a complicated affair, comprising 55 witnesses and over 600 items of evidence. Sheriff Skinner presided at the Perth Courthouse and the public packed the gallery, all keen to see the 84 year-old Lord Barnby giving evidence and the diminutive, eloquent prisoner. Metcalfe's trial, and the eventual verdict, hinged on three crucial factors :

Firstly, Metcalfe's stay in a French prison (which he spoke about at great length) gained him great sympathy with the jury. The conditions had been squalid, especially for a man 'innocent until proven guilty'.

Secondly, Metcalfe was presented to the jury as an honest man, forced to use his own funds to pay accounts owed by Lord Barnby. Witnesses spoke of his generosity and his popularity. He was also able to convince the courthouse that his flight from the country was not through guilt, but due to a sense of fear that his explanation for the 'unusual' accounting at Castle Menzies would not be believed.

Thirdly, and most importantly, Lord Barnby proved to be a thorn in the side of the prosecution. His performance in court was strange, even surreal. Despite the weight of evidence provided by witnesses, he refused to acknowledge that he consistently failed to pay accounts, and that he was unpopular because of it. He seemed more interested in scoring points against the defence council, than in honestly answering questions. Most damningly of all, under cross-examination he refused to accept that the salary he had paid to Metcalfe was insufficient. This refusal, along with futile arguments over the rental value of Metcalfe's house, gave Lord Barnby the appearance of miserliness and an air of pomposity, which did not sit well with the jury.

Finally, after a trial that lasted three days, the jury returned a verdict of "not proven". Sherriff Skinner was forced to silence the cheers from the crowd on three occasions, as the verdict clearly met the approval of the throngs. Francis Metcalfe walked away from Perth Court on Wednesday 3rd May. Not entirely innocent, but not guilty. To the public he was a Robin Hood figure and he immediately took full advantage of the situation – selling his story to The Sunday Post for a substantial figure. The expose of his run from the law and time in a French prison was serialised over four weeks, proving incredibly popular. Metcalfe's articles were well written, even endearing, and clearly written to present a story of a wronged and innocent man.

So, armed with a handsome reward for his newspaper columns, Metcalfe left Aberfeldy and the story of the Castle Menzies Robin Hood was over.

Well, not quite . . .

On moving from Castle Menzies, Metcalfe took lodging in a house called Mayville, on the Crieff Road in Perth. From there he wrote his articles for The Sunday Post and began the hunt for new employment, conscious that his limited funds would not last long. He was fortunate, however, to receive an encouraging reply from George Sellar & Son Ltd, the well known agricultural implements supplier, based in Huntly.

The position of a commercial traveller in farm machinery was ideally suited to Metcalfe, with his experience and contacts within the farming community. He was engaged in late May 1926. Probably unaware of Metcalfe's 1923 conviction, but undoubtedly, fully apprised of his recent brush with the law, John Hunter Turner (the Managing Director of Sellars) was understandably cautious. Metcalfe suggested that he could provide a Bond of Caution, before starting his employment.

Metcalfe, in his new position, would be trusted with handling customer accounts, collecting payments and receiving upfront expenses and monies from his employers. The Bond of Caution was a document signed by previous employers, associates and witnesses, confirming Metcalfe's trustworthiness and guaranteeing his financial security, to the value of

£500. Metcalfe promised to obtain the Bond straight away and began his employment immediately.

However, within a couple of weeks, the Bond had yet to be presented. Mr Turner wrote to Metcalfe and insisted that the document be brought to him. Metcalfe apologised and promised that he would do so. After two further weeks, and several broken promises, Metcalfe at last presented the Bond to Mr Turner, at his home in Alloa. The document contained 13 signatures, some guaranteeing Metcalfe financially, and some as witnesses. Those signing included James Morgan, from the Clydesdale Bank in Aberfeldy, James Miller, coal merchant from Aberfeldy, Duncan MacLean and Christina Scott, who were also both from Aberfeldy. The impressive document satisfied the managing director of George Sellar & Sons, and Metcalfe was allowed to continue with his employment unhindered.

Within a few weeks, however, worrying warning signs began to emerge. The company was forced to post reminders to several customers over the non-payment of accounts. Mr Turner was then contacted by these clients, assuring him that they had all paid their accounts directly to Sellar's representative Francis Metcalfe. Understandably concerned, Mr Turner contacted Metcalfe and insisted that he present himself at the company's head office immediately. In the meantime, he retrieved Metcalfe's Bond of Caution from among his papers and decided to look through it again – this time more carefully. The document, taken on face value, appeared to be genuine, however Mr Turner decided it would be prudent to contact some of the witnesses and guarantors who had signed the paper. He wired or wrote to James Morgan, James Millar, James Simpson and Joseph Hay among others. Their replies came by return. None of the signatories had agreed to sign such a Bond, nor did they even know of its existence. Some of the people named on the document did know Metcalfe, but he had never asked them to sign such a paper and, if asked, they would not have agreed to do so. Perth County police were immediately informed and an audit of the company's books was undertaken. A warrant was, once again, issued for the arrest of Francis Metcalfe on a charge of "fraud and embezzlement". In addition to the fraudulent document, the audit discovered payments of £183 3s 3d (approximately £11,000 today) missing from the business.

The police called on Metcalfe's lodgings on the Crieff Road in Perth, however he had, once again, left in a hurry. A description was hastily issued to other police stations, ports and BBC Radio. Metcalfe was last seen wearing a grey tweed suit, black bowler hat and brown shoes. He was carrying a brown suitcase, containing a blue serge suit, and a black case containing some of Sellar & Son's business ledgers. Of immediate concern to the police was the chance of Metcalfe returning abroad. A special watch was maintained on the ports, however there were no sightings. For the second time in just over a year, a manhunt was underway for Francis

William Metcalfe.

Almost two weeks passed without a sighting until, once again, money proved to be Metcalfe's undoing. A letter to a friend in Perth, pleading for funds, provided the police with Metcalfe's address. This time he had not ventured abroad, but had taken a room at the Caledonian Hotel in Edinburgh, under an assumed name.

Metcalfe, at the time of arrest, had only four shillings in his possession. This time there was to be no escape from the law. Metcalfe pled guilty to the charges and was sentenced at Perth Sheriff's Court to 15 months' imprisonment. Passing sentence, on Valentine's Day 1927, Sheriff Hill-Thomas was staggered at the intricacy of Metcalfe's forgery and the easy way in which lies passed his lips.

There were no cheers from the gallery on this occasion, as the prisoner was led away. Metcalfe was transferred from Perth Prison to the tough Barlinnie Jail in Glasgow to serve his sentence.

Little is known of what became of Francis Metcalfe, following his release from prison in 1928. Perhaps he changed his name? Perhaps he learnt his lesson and led a quiet, law abiding existence?

# THE GRANDTULLY
# MURDER CASE

In the summer of 1901, the concerns of the population in Highland Perthshire were focused thousands of miles away, as The Boer War raged in Southern Africa. Many of the valley's young men had volunteered for The Black Watch Regiment and were about to be shipped to South Africa.

For a short time, however, another news story was the principle topic of conversation in the area. The brutal and fatal murder of a young woman in the peaceful village of Grandtully, situated on the banks of the River Tay, midway between Aberfeldy and Ballinluig.

Early in the morning on Friday 2nd August at about 9am, Gordon Michie, a cattle drover, employed at Grandtully Hill Farm, decided to inspect the small path that ran from opposite the Grandtully Hotel down to the river's edge. He frequently used the path to water the cows in hot weather. Recently there had been travellers (or tinkers as they were then called) camping in one of the plantation fields nearby. He had seen the light from their fires the previous evening

and knew they frequented the Grandtully Hotel. After
leaving the public house they would stagger along
the path, habitually smashing glasses and bottles. Mr
Michie was often required to clear broken glass from
the path, in order to ensure safe passage to the water's
edge for his herd. The reputation of the travellers was
notorious locally, and their frequent appearance in the
summer months always caused concern to the villagers.

Next to the Old Mill and the Salmon House the path
led through a small plantation, where the travellers
had been camping, down the bank to the edge of the
river. As Michie walked down the path he noticed
some discarded food and a smashed cup. He was not
surprised, he had expected to find some debris. He
picked up the smashed cup and walked on toward the
river. The plantation was not wide and just 20 feet away
over a small wall. He noticed a plaid shawl lying loose
on the ground. It did not seem in a poor condition,
the usual sort of item that might be thrown away. It
was close to the river and could have been tossed over
the wall, and down the bank, from the road. As he
walked on, he noticed a bundle of cloths. Michie half
expected to find a drunk vagrant, sleeping off the
previous night's excesses.  Then his eyes were drawn
to a body lying on the ground. The face was blackened
on one side and heavily bruised and disfigured. He
knew at once it was the body of a dead woman. She
lay on her back, one arm across her chest, the other
stretched out to the side. Her body was approximately
5 feet from the fast running river's edge, which is

shallow on that bank, and just over 20 feet from the road. Had her body entered the water, it may well never have been found. The initial impression was that she may have fallen, or been pushed, and rolled down the bank. Only the hollow of a tree stump preventing her body from slipping into the river.

THE SCENE OF THE CRIME

X WHERE THE BODY WAS DISCOVERED.

Hastening up the slope, through the oak coppice, to the road he saw Sergeant George Strathearn, the local volunteer drill instructor, cycling to Dunkeld. Michie and the Sergeant covered the body with the shawl, to keep the flies at bay. Sergeant Strathearn immediately set off for Ballinluig, on his bicycle, to fetch Constable Grant. The doctor in Aberfeldy was wired for, and Michie stayed to await their arrival.

An inspection of the ground around the body revealed marks in the earth, probably showing that the body had been dragged into its current position or pushed down the slope. Constable Grant had wired for Sergeant Small, from Pitlochry, and Sergeant Campbell, from Aberfeldy, and the party retraced the drag marks in the ground which led them up the bank, over the small wall, and across the road. There was evidence of a campfire in the field, on the other side of the road, and a trail of items discarded on the roadside, between the Sawmill Cottage and the crime scene, and at the campsite. Cooking tins were found, which left the impression the party had left in a hurry (cooking utensils were expensive, and unlikely to have been left behind), some balls of wool, a bundle of canes, a whisky bottle and a man's cap. Also located nearer the body was a torn piece of a woman's coat. John Stewart, who was the tenant at Sawmill Cottage and knew the area well, joined the search. The party also discovered a woman's handkerchief which was folded and contained a number of tansy roots (roots from the tansy flower were used for a wide range of medicinal purposes, including inducing abortion, preventing intestinal worms, and repelling insects). The impression everyone had was that a violent argument had taken place.

A horse and cart were summoned, and the body was removed to the local morgue, which was attached to the Combination Poorhouse at Logierait. Once at the morgue, it was obvious that the matter was a more serious one than had initially been thought. The Chief Constable MacPherson, of the Perth County Constabulary immediately summoned Dr Beatty, from Pitlochry, to perform an initial examination, and despatched Inspector Campbell to take over the investigation.

Dr Beatty began his autopsy at 8pm. His initial findings, recorded in his report, were as follows:

*Deceased appears to be about 35 years of age. She was 5 feet 6 inches in height, had dark hair, and was fairly well dressed with a yellow shawl, grey jacket, dark shirt, and lacing boots with tackets in sole.*

*The face was badly hashed, all the injuries, it is believed, having been caused by kicking or other similar harsh treatment at the hands of person, or persons, unknown.*

Even though the hour was now late, the full autopsy was ordered immediately. The findings of the initial examination were noted by the police officers in attendance, then Dr Beatty and Dr Mackay, called from Aberfeldy, began the gruesome procedure. The injuries to the body were extensive. Her clothing was heavily bloodstained on the rear. The pupils were dislocated, and the face covered in blood. On the victim's head were five puncture wounds that had penetrated the scalp, right through to the bone. On her forehead was a large abrasion, as if she had been held down by the sole of a boot. Her jaw and the left side of her face were covered in abrasions and wounds. Her nose, teeth and lips had been flattened by repeated blows which, the doctors surmised, had been delivered with a clenched fist. On turning the victim's body over the doctors were faced with an injury even larger than any of those on the face or neck. A large puncture wound to the lower torso had been inflicted with great force. The weapon used, most likely a knife, had then been pulled downwards, through the body, to leave a gaping wound which had bled profusely. The legs and feet were covered with grass and mud, probably indicating that the body had been dragged to its final resting place. Both doctors agreed that the bruises and abrasions to the body had all been delivered – with some force – by repeated kicks and by a clenched fist. The puncture wounds had doubtless been caused by a knife. Later, under cross-examination, neither doctor was of the opinion that the injuries could have been caused by falling or by hitting a branch or tree stump, whilst accidently tumbling down the bank.

The police were surprised when a gentleman from Pitlochry turned up at the mortuary. He had heard the story of a woman's body being found and was anxious because his wife had not returned home on the previous night. He was allowed to see the body, however it was not his missing wife.

Meanwhile the police had not been idle. It appeared that a group of itinerant travellers had been camping in the field just 200 yards from Grandtully, close to where the body was found. The group, consisting of three men and a woman, had been drinking in the Grandtully Hotel, both on the night of the murder, and on the previous evening. They had persuaded David Paterson, a cattle drover aged 68 of no fixed abode, to part with a shilling for whisky. He, and two others, had spent time drinking and talking with the three travellers. Paterson bought a beer for the woman, who called herself Jessie and told him that she came from Alyth. She invited the men back to their campsite, offering to boil some water for tea. Paterson wanted his shilling back, so agreed to accompany them.

On the evening of the murder, around 10.15pm, two witnesses, James Thomson and John Robertson, had been returning from Logeirait to Grandtully along the road and had to pass the camp. They were somewhat nervous as the reputation of the group was notorious in the village. Indeed, the majority of locals kept their distance, particularly at night. They heard noises and, noticing the camp fire, they (somewhat bravely) remarked to the small group:

"You had better shift, you are not to camp here".

One of the men stepped forward, he was brandishing a knife, "I will be damned if I'll shift!"

The travellers asked for a smoke, but the witnesses replied that they didn't smoke. This seemed to irritate the man, who then asked for a shilling to buy some whisky from the hotel. Thomson and Robertson, who wisely wanted to extract themselves from an unpleasant encounter with an armed man, parted with a shilling and made they way hurriedly away from the scene, heading towards Grandtully.

The three men, David Urquhart (sometimes called Smith), John Foye and a third man named Mitchell (first name unknown), now had a shilling, which could be used for more whisky. Urquhart gave the coin to Jessie and sent her back along the road to the hotel to buy a bottle.

An hour or so later two further witnesses, John Stewart, from the Sawmill Cottage, and Jane Anderson, from Portnasallan Ferry Cottage at Logierait, passed the lady sat on the edge of the road. There was a nearly empty whisky bottle beside her. Obviously the worse for drink, they helped her to the other side of the road. The men from the campsite came and took her away, in the direction of their camping ground.

Around midnight, after Jane Anderson had returned to Logierait, she overheard the sound of footsteps hurrying past her door, in the direction of Ballinluig.

Descriptions of the three men, and of the victim, were circulated to all the local Police Stations and Post Offices. Urquhart was about 40 years of age, stoutly built with dark hair and a dark complexion, Mitchell about 60 with grey whiskers, and Foye about 30 and well built. The identity of the woman's body was soon resolved. Isabella Grieve, from Inchture, recognised the woman as her daughter Jessie. Isabella Grieve had little involvement in her daughter's upbringing though, her own mother had taken over the role. Jessie had taken the name Lawson, but in September 1890 had married a labourer from Alyth, named Peter Smith.

Their marriage lasted eight or nine years, however, Jessie had a habit of disappearing for long periods of time. Her absences usually involved heavy drinking. She would travel with a group of tramps, sleeping in camps, before returning to Peter Smith's door at Cairnleith Place in Alyth. He could not understand her behaviour, but he told the police:

"I always let her in when she returned, but I could make nothing of her." He also added, "She was a woman who would have lived with any man who would give her drink."

Peter Smith had identified Jessie from the photograph circulated by the police, but on arriving at the Logierait Poorhouse, was unable to recognise her body, due to the bruising and blackening on her face.

Two of the men, Mitchell and Foye, had travelled across country, to avoid the roads, spending one night sleeping in Pitlochry Distillery. On reaching the village of Straloch, half-way between Pitlochry and Kirkmichael, they both entered the village inn and bought a drink. The Landlord recognised them from the description and was immediately suspicious of their demeanour, as was the local police constable. At the beginning of the 20th century it was unusual to see strangers in the village and their appearance was noticed by everyone in the room. Whilst extra constables were sent for, both men slipped away, but were found hiding in a barn near the inn and were promptly arrested.

Mitchell and Foye told the police they had separated from David Urquhart at Grandtully. Checkpoints were set up on all the local crossroads and search parties were organised. A description of Urquhart was issued, in the hope he would spotted by someone.

At around midnight on Saturday 3rd August, leading

into the morning of Sunday 4th, police constable John Grant left Logierait and headed towards Ballinluig on his bicycle. At the junction of the Great North Road and the hill in Ballinluig he questioned two young men he had spotted standing there. He knew that Mitchell and Foye had already been arrested at Straloch, so he was on the lookout for the third man Urquhart (or Smith as he sometimes called himself). As he did so he heard footsteps behind him, as he turned around, he saw another man walking towards him. The stranger was shabbily dressed in a grey jacket, no cap and a handkerchief draped over his head and fastened under his chin. PC Grant leaned forward over his bicycle and asked the man:

"Where are you going?"

There was no answer. The constable challenged him again, "Where have you come from?"

The man replied "I have been sleeping in the wood near Grandtully since Friday morning."

He seemed agitated or excited. PC Grant asked him: "Where is your cap?" (It was almost unknown at that time to see a man in public without a cap or hat of some kind, even in summer)

"I lost it on the road near Grandtully on Thursday night." After a pause he then added, "I suppose you are looking for me?"

PC Grant answered, "Or a man like you."

The constable removed the handkerchief from the

man's head, in order to get a better look at his face. One of the other men there lit a match, so they could all make out his face more clearly. From the description given to the police by Mitchell and Foye, PC Grant immediately knew it was the man they were searching for.

"What is your name?" he asked.

"My name is David Smith. I give myself up. You have all the roads watched, I cannot get away."

PC Grant cautioned the man, "I am taking you on suspicion, anything you might say may be used in evidence against you."

Smith (or Urquhart) responded, "There were three men there, I didn't do it."

Smith was arrested and escorted back through Logierait to be questioned at Aberfeldy. As PC Grant and the prisoner made their way to Grandtully, Smith pointed to the spot, in the hills above the railway bridge, where he had been hiding. As they passed the point at which the body had been found, Smith put his head in his hands, mumbling to himself, "I have done for myself now."

Smith was shown a man's cap, which had been found near to the body. He said it was his and that he had lost it on the road, somewhere near to Grandtully.

On 18th August PC Grant, accompanied by Dr Beattie, conducted another search of the ground near to the spot that Jessie Lawson's body had been found. They found a knife, just a few feet from the body. It was hidden in the undergrowth and the grass had grown around it, making it difficult to spot. Dr Beattie was certain it was the type of implement that could have caused the wounds on the deceased's body.

All three men were kept in prison for a considerable period of time. Mitchell and Foye were released after 4 weeks but, it was agreed, would appear in court as witnesses for the prosecution. In Perth, for the first time in five years, a High Court of The Justiciary was arranged, and convened on Monday 15th October 1901.

Lord Kincairney presided over a packed courthouse, as David Urquhart (sometimes known as Smith) was charged with the following crimes:

*1) In August, or September, 1900 in the turnip shed at the farm of Drumhead, near Blairgowrie, assaulted Jessie Lawson, or Smith, wife of Peter Smith, labourer, Cairnleith Place, Alyth, by striking her with his fists.*

*2) In October 1900, in the farmhouse of Forehill, in the Parish of Caputh, did assault Jessie Lawson, or Smith, by kicking her, and*

*3) On the 1st or 2nd August 1901 at, or near, the part of the road leading from Grandtully to Dunkeld, and about half a mile from Grandtully, struck Jessie Lawson, or Smith, on her face with his fists, and inflicted injuries upon her head and private parts with a knife, or other instrument, kicking her on the face, arms and legs, and murdering her.*

The lesser charges of assault were dropped in favour of the more serious charge of murder. Although pleading not guilty to murder, the mere mention of the previous assault charges would have been enough to give the jury a strong impression of Urquhart's previous character. The trial, which lasted just two days, saw several witnesses called for the prosecution. The inn keeper, from the Grandtully Hotel, Angus MacDonald, and his daughter Nellie, recognised the accused and confirmed his presence in their hotel on the night of Jessie's murder. He also confirmed that they had been drinking. The two men previously arrested, Mitchell and Foye, testified to the court that they had left the scene, along with George Paterson the cattle drover, whilst Urquhart and Jessie were arguing, and (when arrested) had no idea that she had been killed. They both claimed that they had only met again, by accident, the following day in Moulin. George Paterson told the court that Mitchell said to him "That woman will get bad play tonight; she will be abused, and you had better get away, or you will get yourself into trouble."

Urquhart's apparent confession to PC Grant, whilst being taken to Aberfeldy, was heavily relied upon by the prosecution, despite the defence's objection that it had not been spoken in front of witnesses.

Several witnesses from Grandtully recalled hearing the noise of an argument coming from the camp on that night, but none could recall hearing a woman screaming or in distress.

Another witness, John MacDonald from Balnaguard, remembered meeting Urquhart late on Saturday evening on the road, near his home in Balnaguard. Urquhart, wearing a handkerchief on his head, asked MacDonald if he had a spare cap he could give him. Urquhart claimed he had got drunk and lost his in Grandtully Wood on the previous evening. When MacDonald mentioned the murder to Urquhart, he claimed to have no knowledge of it.

The medical evidence followed. Dr Beattie described the injuries in graphic detail, which would certainly have had the most profound effect on the jury. In fact, one jury member fainted and had to be escorted from the room.

The cap, found at the scene, was produced and shown to Urquhart. He recognised it as his own. Dr Beattie also confirmed that the accused's boots matched the impressions left on Jessie's torso and forehead.

Acting for the defence Mr Guy struggled to raise any doubt in the jury's minds. On cross-examination, Dr Beattie was certain none of the injuries could have been caused by an accidental fall. Urquhart's demeanour during the trial had been sullen and detached. Mr Guy reminded the jury that Urquhart had been very cooperative during his arrest and questioning. When originally arrested there were no blood stains on his clothes and there were no spots of blood on the knife either.

However, many hours had passed before his arrest,

giving him ample opportunity to change his attire, and dispose of the clothes he had been wearing on the Friday evening. The knife too, had lain in the grass for several days and any tell-tale marks would have been washed away by the rain.

Without the certainties provided by modern forensics, juries and judges of the period placed understandable weight on the statements of witnesses. Perhaps less fathomable to our modern eye, is just how much the conduct, behaviour and social class of the victim and accused was taken into account.

David Uquhart stood in the dock, as the jury returned, his face moist with sweat and his hands shaking palpably. However, it was noticed by all in the court, a great load seemed to be lifted from his mind when the jury returned a verdict of culpable homicide, and not murder.

Once again, drinking had been a mitigating circumstance in Urquhart's behaviour, rather than a contributing factor. To the respectable middle-class jury of the day, the drunken conduct of Jessie Lawson had been beneath contempt. By drinking the bottle of whisky, purchased from the Grandtully Hotel, instead of returning to the camp with it, she had somehow contributed to the murderous attack.

Lord Kincairney had no doubt, however, as to the seriousness of the crime. Stating in court that: "it is one of the worst cases of culpable homicide that has ever come before me." He sentenced Urquhart to 12 years penal servitude and the prisoner was led from the court.

Newspaper reporters, present at the trial, all reported that the crowded courtroom cleared quickly, following the pronouncement, and the public all felt satisfied with the result.

The reaction of Jessie Lawson's husband and mother to the verdict was not recorded.

****

As a footnote to this sad story, Jessie Lawson, or Smith, was buried at Logierait Church, where she, and other paupers, often slept during the summer months.

Sergeant Strathearn, the local volunteer Drill Instructor, who was the second witness on the scene, was to be part – just 12 months later -in another story featured in this book.

Lastly, and perhaps most tragically of all, undisclosed to the jury at the time of the trial, was David Urquhart's previous conviction. In 1883, whilst still a young man, he had been sentenced to 21 year's penal servitude for the culpable homicide of his 2-year-old daughter. Living in Dundee and working in the docks, he rented a room in a boarding house with his wife. One evening, whilst under the influence of drink, he beat his daughter so savagely that she sadly died from her injuries. The attack was so sickening that the details do not bear repeating.

He had been released from prison just a few months before his first attack on Jessie Lawson, and just 18 months before killing her.

# COINCIDENCE AND SUPERNATURAL ASSISTANCE

Sergeant George Strathearn, who featured in the earlier chapter about the killing of Jessie Lawson, was – by bizarre coincidence - to also figure in another strange and tragic case, just 12 months later.

On the evening of Sunday 26th October 1902, the local drill instructor, was sat in front of the fire, at home in the parlour of his cottage in Aberfeldy. The clock on the mantelpiece had just struck 8 o'clock. His wife got up, excused herself, put on her house slippers and left the house quietly by the back door. Sergeant Strathearn thought nothing of it. Perhaps she was merely putting the ashes in the bin? After all, she was just wearing a black shirt and top, no hat, coat or boots.

After half an hour, however, she had not returned. Sergeant Strathearn stepped outside, but there was no sign of her. He made enquiries with his neighbours and paced the street, but she was nowhere to be seen. The following morning, with the advent of daylight, search parties were organised. Searches were carried out throughout the hills, wood and glens of the valley. Both banks of the River Tay were diligently scoured, and several boats joined the search along the river. Heavy rain, during recent days, had swollen the river and it was feared that if Mrs Strathearn's body had entered the river it could have been washed away.

Her description was issued to the local newspapers:

*Mrs Strathearn is about 36 years of age, a little over 5 feet in height, and of medium build. Her hair is of a reddish colour, and her face round and full. When she left home she was dressed in a black shirt, black bodice, with waist belt. She wore a pair of house slippers.*

She had suffered illness during the summer, and it appeared that she may not have fully recovered. Her actions and words, on occasions, appeared strange. However, no one had expected her to behave dangerously or recklessly.

A week passed and there were no sightings. Had Mrs Strathearn taken her own life? Had she accidentally slipped and fallen into the river? Had the many travellers, that frequented the district, abducted or killed her? On Sunday 2nd November more than 200 people took the unusual measure to ignore the sabbath and organise another search. Both banks of the river were searched for several miles, but no body was sighted, or any clues found.

As the weeks passed by the residents of Aberfeldy feared that the mystery of Mrs Strathearn's disappearance would never be solved. A month later, however, Sergeant Strathearn received a letter in the post, from a lady called Rachel Cameron, who resided at Rannoch. The letter contained the simple message:

"the body would be found high and dry on the banks of the river."

Sergeant Strathearn was naturally dubious and surprised by this unexpected communication. He chose to ignore it. Another week followed and he received a further communication from Rachel Cameron. However, this time the message contained far more detailed information. Once again, it was stated that the body would be found high and dry on the bank of the river. What followed next was a careful account, giving a description of the exact spot in which Mrs Strathearn's body would be discovered:

"It is to be found lying on the bank, near a house somewhat similar in shape, but having taller chimneys, to the house in Rannoch where I reside, and it will be discovered near well-kept gardens. A fallen tree will be near the spot."

This, and other descriptive details, enabled Sergeant Strathearn to persuade the police to organise another search. Almost two months had now passed; however, the remarkable letter, and the reputation of Rachel Cameron, were enough to convince the authorities to reopen the hunt.

In addition to the missing Mrs Strathearn, another mystery now presented itself. Just who was Rachel Cameron and why did the authorities place so much importance in her letter?

There was an ancient belief in the Highlands, and in parts of Europe and Canada, that the seventh daughter of a seventh daughter, or the red headed daughter of a red headed mother,  possessed the power of second sight (prophetic vision). Even as the twentieth century began, many still believed in this mystic power. Indeed, following Sergeant Strathearn's receipt of the letter, *The Courier* newspaper sent a special correspondent to investigate the story.

In the nineteenth century Rachel Cameron lived beside Loch Rannoch, near to Bridge of Gaur. She had red hair and possessed the gift of second sight. It was a gift that had been with her family for generations and was passed down through the seventh daughters. The ability often brought with it pain and exhaustion, but it was also a gift that she used to bring comfort to those in distress.

In 1896 a youth was drowned in Loch Awe but the body could not be found. A friend of the family remembering Rachel's reputation went to visit her and seek her help. That night Rachel had a vision and awoke exhausted and bathed in sweat. She told the friend that the mother must go to a certain island on the Loch, and there line herself up with two other islands and a hill on the mainland.

The next day, the mother was rowed across to an island that matched the description given by Rachel Cameron. She walked along the shore until she could glimpse the hill and the other two islands. Suddenly there was a disturbance on the water and her son's body came to the surface and floated towards her. The boy was later buried at Innischaill, the island in Loch Awe where the mother had first glimpsed the body.

Rachel herself died the following year but left a daughter, also called Rachel Cameron, also red haired and who also possessed the gift of second sight. In one famous case, a farmer from Aberfeldy disappeared on his way home and was suspected of having fallen into the River Tay. But, although the river was repeatedly searched, no trace of his body could be found. In desperation Rachel Cameron the younger was consulted. She 'saw' the body held in a tree beneath a strange looking bridge which she sketched. It was, of course, Wade's Bridge at Aberfeldy. When divers searched under the bridge, they found the farmer's body trapped among the roots of a tree. In another case she was consulted over the mysterious death of a gamekeeper. She immediately described where his clothes would be found and declared that poachers had killed him. A poacher was arrested soon after and admitted the crime. A search revealed his clothes in the area described by Rachel Cameron. There were many examples of "second sight" recorded in the Highlands, during the 18th and 19th centuries. The occurrences were treated seriously and with reverence, so much so, that in 1894, and again in 1902, the Royal Society for Psychical Research travelled to the Highlands in an attempt to document examples.

Armed with the description in the letter, and Rachel Cameron's formidable reputation, Sergeant Strathearn accompanied the final search party, as they hunted the banks of the River Tay for an area that matched the one described in the letter. The search party, including Sergeant Strathearn, were all sceptical of the second sight claims. However, they were completely stunned, on December 10th 1902, when their search revealed Mrs Strathearn's body in circumstances exactly matching those described in the letter. Everyone in the party remained at the spot near Kindallachan, after the body was removed, to fully contemplate the situation. They were stunned at how exactly Rachel Cameron's vision had matched the site at which the body was discovered. All reported that they had changed their opinion on the gift of second sight.

Sadly, Mrs Strathearn's body was badly decomposed and no cause of death could be ascertained. What really happened to her on that fateful night will never be known.

George Strathearn retired from his role as drill instructor with the Black Watch Volunteers in 1910. He was presented with a silver coffee pot, at a special ceremony in Aberfeldy, by friends and ex-members of the Volunteers, many of whom had taken part in the search for his wife's body eight years earlier.

The younger Rachel Cameron died in 1914 and both mother and daughter are buried in the now abandoned, tranquil and peaceful graveyard at Killichonan by Loch Rannoch.

Just before her death her opinion was sought on The Great War (in which hostilities had just begun). She answered: "there will be a great loss of life."

# THE TOWER
# COTTAGE MURDER

A little after 8am on the morning of Friday 26th September 1947, one of the most violent crimes in Scottish history took place in a peaceful cottage in rural Perthshire.

The war had finished, just two years earlier, and the communities of Aberfeldy and Kenmore were gradually returning to normal. For many people life continued as usual, yet the residual effects of the conflict lived on. Rationing was still in place and, in Kenmore, Polish soldiers were still stationed at Taymouth Castle.

On the expansive Bolfracks Estate among the trees, on the hills overlooking Taymouth Castle, stood the White Tower. The McIntyre family lived in a cottage (known as Tower Cottage, or The Towers) attached to the impressive Gothic structure.

Peter McIntyre had been head shepherd on the

estate since 1935, and had set off early for Perth
that morning, to attend the Perth sheep sales. He
had recently received his three-monthly pay packet
(around £80 – approximately £3,000 today) and left
it with his wife, Catherine. Aged 47, she also helped
on the estate, cleaning and cooking at the big house.
Archie, their son, aged 22, was employed on a nearby
estate and was hoping to join the Police force. Mary,
their 16-year-old daughter, worked as a typist in the
Commercial Bank in Aberfeldy, and had already left
for work. Alone in the cottage, Catherine McIntyre
(known as Cathie) had a short time before she was
due to go and light the fires at Tombuie, the house
belonging to Mr J Douglas Hutchinson, the owner of
the estate. He was expected for a weekend of stalking,
after having attended the Perth Hunt. Cathie stacked
the breakfast dishes, ready to wash, and sat down to
write two letters to her grown up daughters. Cathie
glanced at the clock, knowing that if she finished the
letters by 10 o'clock, she could hand them to the local
postman John Shearer, who usually called at that time.

As Cathie sat down to begin writing, outside the
cottage, in the tall bracken that bordered the track
running down the hill, there was a sudden movement.
A small, unkempt man, nervously gripping a shotgun
in his hand, had been hidden in the undergrowth for
several hours. He had been carefully watching the
house, waiting for Peter McIntyre, Archie and Mary
to leave for work. Mary was last to leave, at 8.35am.
Once he was certain they would not return, he made

his move. The family had five dogs. Four were working dogs but were safely in their kennels. The fifth, a docile pet was in the cottage with Cathie. Perhaps the dogs barked, on seeing the unkempt stranger, or perhaps Cathie opened the door on hearing a noise. Did he knock at the door, or force his way in? It is unlikely the door was locked, in any case.

At 4.30pm John Keay, from Home Street in Aberfeldy, had arrived to deliver coal. The family's pet dog ran past him as he drove up the track. He found the door locked and left.

Archie returned to the house at 5.15pm, he was surprised to find the doors locked, the family's cairn terrier sat outside, and his mother apparently not at home. The postman, John Shearer, had called at 11.30am, and discovering the house locked, he had left the newspaper and post on the step. Archie then remembered that his mother was due to set the fires at Tombuie and was probably still there. He sat down on the step to read the newspaper.

Shortly afterwards at 5.30pm, however, the estate gamekeeper Clement McKercher arrived at the cottage and told Archie that he could see no smoke coming from the chimneys at Tombuie. He wondered why Cathie had not been to light the fires? She was also expected to visit McKercher's wife for a cup of tea and had not done so. McKercher had lent Cathie his watch, the previous evening, as her watch was not working, so there was no reason for her to be late. At this point Archie began to worry. He could not get

into the cottage, as the doors were locked, so climbed
in through the kitchen window. On the kitchen table
lay Cathie's glasses and the unfinished letters she
had begun in the morning. There was no sign of his
mother. He searched the house and was surprised to
find his own bedroom door locked. Unable to find any
keys, he took a wood axe, that was stored by the front
door, and forced the bedroom door open. As he did
so, Archie was met by a gruesome and shocking sight.
His mother lay on the bed, her body covered with a
mattress, dragged from the other bed in the room.
A scarf covered her face, and aprons had been tied
around her neck. Her hands had been secured across
her stomach with black bootlaces and her head had
been savagely bludgeoned. Cathie's face was swollen
and discoloured. Archie immediately sent McKercher
to call for the police. There were no keys in the house,
it appeared that the assailant had locked the doors and
taken the keys with him.

The matter was immediately identified as a serious
one, and Chief Constable Sim, of the Perth County
Police, together with several officers attended the
scene. It was discovered, that £80 (in £5 notes),
rationing coupons, Cathie's wedding ring, and a grey/
blue man's suit had been stolen from the cottage.

Dr Charles Swanson, from Aberfeldy, was called to
examine the body. The doctor and the police officers
were forced to break the glass panel in the front door
and climb into the cottage. He estimated the time of
death between 9am and 10am.

Meanwhile, the police began a widespread search of the surrounding countryside. It was initially suspected that a tramp or vagrant, passing through, might be to blame. However this line of enquiry was quickly dropped, when Archie McIntyre explained to the police that he had the impression someone may have been moving in the bracken, near to the cottage, as he had walked down the track to work earlier that morning. He had dismissed it, however, as he had needed to get to work, and thought it may have been just a deer. The police immediately searched the undergrowth in the area McIntyre described. They found an area of flattened foliage, indicating that someone had been lying there for a considerable time.

A further search of the hillside, approximately 400 yards from the cottage, revealed an area of tumbled stones in which the police found blood stained overalls, a dirty raincoat, two shotgun cartridges and a sawn off shotgun. Smears of blood on the butt of the

shotgun indicated it was probably the murder weapon. The police also discovered several other key items that would help connect their owner to the murder. A blood-stained handkerchief, a safety razor (with hair still stuck to the blade) and a key piece of evidence – the return section of a railway ticket, issued the previous day, for a journey from Perth to

Aberfeldy. Crucially, the ticket was of a special type, only issued to soldiers in uniform.

The revelation of the railway ticket helped the police narrow the search significantly. Interest now fell on Taymouth Castle, lying just below the cottage, in the valley. Upwards of 800 Polish soldiers were still billeted there. Police enquires at the Castle did not produce any results.

However, along with other witnesses, John Moir, owner of the general merchants shop in Kenmore Square, saw a scruffy looking man at around 11.45am. The man, who clearly did not speak much English, was enquiring about the times of buses to Aberfeldy. Wilhelm Horn (a German prisoner-of-war, working nearby) also spotted the man, anxiously clutching a satchel, waiting for the bus.

Janet Pringle, from Acharn, the conductress on the bus from Killin to Aberfeldy also witnessed a scruffy looking Polish man board the noon bus at Kenmore. Witnesses in Aberfeldy were also able to describe a man who took a taxi from Aberfeldy to Perth that day. The taxi driver remembered that the man paid the fare from a roll of banknotes. From the various witness statements, a detailed description, together with details of the murder weapon, was issued without delay:

"About 35 years of age, slim build, thin face, pointed chin and clean shaven, suffers from a spasmodic cough"

A Mrs Isabella Milne, from Tulloch Farm in

Aberdeenshire, immediately recognised the description of the shotgun and of the man. She told the police that a Polish ex-soldier called Stanislaw Myszka had worked on the farm from June until September 5th. He had told the family that he was going to travel to the Perth area to search for work. Shortly after he left the farm, it was noticed that a shotgun had gone missing. A Scottish girl, married to a Polish soldier from Taymouth Castle, remembered Myszka suddenly appearing, flush with cash.

With a name to match their description, the police intensified their manhunt. During the morning of 2nd October, the police were searching disused RAF buildings, at Longside near Peterhead. Constable McLaren saw a man running from one of the huts across the fields. The officers immediately gave chase. After three quarters of a mile they apprehended the man, who was attempting to hide under a bush. In his possession were six £5 notes, three £1 notes, 10 shilling and 9d in coins and a number of rationing coupons. When asked his name the man simply replied "Myszka". Mrs McIntyre's wedding ring was found hidden in the insole of his shoe.

Myszka's appearance was not that of the monster that had been built up in the public's imagination. He was a small, insignificant man, dressed in an ill-fitting suit, only 5 feet 2 inches in height.

A trial date was set for January 1948 at Perth. Interest in the case was high and queues formed outside the courthouse, with members of the public anxious to witness proceedings. Myszka pleaded not guilty to murder, but guilty to the theft of the shotgun. As the evidence against him mounted, he lodged a plea of insanity. His counsel argued that he had received upsetting news about his children in France, coupled with three days of sleeplessness and lack of food. His claim, however, was quickly dismissed. Dr Jan Levberg, from the Argyll & Bute Mental Hospital examined Myszka, concluding that he was co-operative and coherent and almost certainly sane at the time of the murder. The crime was clearly for gain and the presence of the shotgun showed premeditation. As well as the evidence of eyewitnesses, the shotgun was recognised by Mrs Milne, who also identified the blood-stained handkerchief, found at the scene, as one she had given to Myszka. The presence of the money, the wedding ring, the railway ticket and the clothing coupons were compounded by the diligence of Professor John Glaister, from Glasgow University's Forensic Sciences Department. He was able to prove – long before the availability of DNA evidence - that hairs found on the safety razor almost certainly matched hairs taken from Myszka's prison razor.

The Jury retired and took less than 20 minutes to reach their verdict. Myszka was found guilty of murder and sentenced to death by hanging. Albert Pierrepoint, the famous hangman, journeyed from London to Perth Prison to undertake his grim task. It was to be the first execution at Perth since 1909 and the only execution of a foreigner on Scottish soil in the 20th Century. It would also prove to be the final execution to take place at Perth prison. A group of 12 people gathered outside the prison, including four women. Following the execution, a notice was pinned to the gate, stating that Myszka's life had been ended at 8.02am. He had proceeded calmly to the scaffold, saying nothing, and making no last-minute requests. Myszka's body was buried within the grounds of the prison.

Stanislaw Myszka, aged 36, had come to the UK in 1945, after spending a number of years in France, during which time he had married a Parisian lady. She gave birth to two daughters. During the early years of the German occupation he had worked as a farm labourer and then in the Nazi labour camps. Following the liberation, he had joined the Polish Resettlement Corp and been stationed at Comrie. It appears that he deserted from there and became a farm labourer in Aberdeenshire. Desperately short of money, and perhaps to fund moving his family from France to Poland, he had undertaken the vicious attack on Cathie Mcintyre. As Myszka had only travelled from Perth the previous day, exactly how he knew about the presence of a large amount of money in the lonely cottage remains a mystery. Local speculation seemed to think that 'pub talk' may have been the reason.

However, whatever his actual motivation, Myszka carried it with him silently to the gallows. The real reason will probably never be known.

His body was buried, without ceremony, in a spot 8' 4" from the corner of the north boundary wall of the prison, next to the bodies of other notorious killers.

# THE LOST SHEPHERD

On the 15th December 1898, the American and Spanish governments signed the Treaty Of Paris, ending the American-Spanish War. In the bustling market town of Aberfeldy, however, things continued as normal, unaffected by world events.

John McLaren, a shepherd from Glenquaich, finished his business at the Aberfeldy Cattle Market. Dusk was falling and McLaren was anxious to make the long journey home before darkness enveloped the Kenmore Road, and the biting cold set in. He made his deposits and necessary withdrawals from the Commercial Bank in the town, thrust the receipts into his pocket-book, and began the long walk westward towards Kenmore. With just his collar turned against the cold and his walking stick for company, he was glad to be joined by a Loch Tayside farmer (also returning from the market), for the long journey home. They chatted until parting ways at the crossroads in Kenmore.

The farmer headed to the north side of the Loch, through Kenmore. McLaren was last seen – by further witnesses – beginning his climb up the steep and winding Glenquaich road at about 6pm. By this time of day in December, it would already be dark, but McLaren, being a shepherd, was used to the walk and the moonlit nights.

He was never seen alive again.

His employer, Miss Cameron from Garrows on the Glenquaich Road, became concerned when he did not return during the evening. She reported him missing the following morning. A search was immediately organised, and a party scoured the hillside road and the nearby woodland. Initial worries were that McLaren had fallen, and perhaps was lying along the steep roadside. Although aged 64, he was fit and robust, after a lifetime of working among the hill farms of Loch Tayside.

No evidence was found, until shortly before dusk when one of the party spotted a collection of discarded items scattered at the roadside, approximately three quarters of a mile above Kenmore. Discovered were a small pocket-knife (which was recognised as belonging to John McLaren), his treasured walking stick and some matches. As night was now drawing in a more detailed and wide-ranging search was hastily organised for the approaching weekend. Search parties combed the hillside and arrangements were made to drain a small, close-by artificial lake, Lochanalarach, as well as drag the water of Loch Tay, close to Kenmore Pier, by boat.

All efforts were fruitless however, and the mystery deepened. McLaren, it became apparent, was carrying a good deal of money in his pocket book (in the form of cash and deposit receipts), yet this was not found among the items discovered at the roadside. The days passed and an appeal was made through the Perthshire Courier, however this too yielded no response.

The mystery offered up no further clues until suddenly, eight days later, at midday on Friday December 23rd, a body was spotted on the stony beach at the south eastern corner of Loch Tay, at Kenmore. The body was wet, but not soaking, and bore no outward marks of violence. In the pockets were some receipted accounts, some loose change but no sign of the pocket-book containing the substantial amount of money McLaren was thought to be carrying. No other clues were found at the scene. The water is shallow at that point, and it seemed unlikely that anyone could drown there.

So exactly what did happen to John McLaren?

An accident seemed unlikely. There was no reason for McLaren to be at the water's edge. The roadway was well above, and set back from, the Loch, and, besides, McLaren had already been seen beginning the ascent up to Glenquaich. He was not a drunkard and was well respected locally. His employer, Miss Cameron, had trusted him to transact business on her behalf in Aberfeldy.

Had he been seen in Aberfeldy carrying a large sum of money and, perhaps, followed? The journey back to Kenmore was at least six miles, surely too long a distance not to notice someone following? Yet how did several of his possessions end up on the roadside three quarters of a mile from where his body was discovered? Surely he would not have walked all the way back to the Loch, for no apparent reason, on such a dark and cold night – and without his walking stick?

Did he see someone on the roadside and fear for his safety? Perhaps turning around to avoid being seen. Why did he stop and light so many matches? Was he looking for something, or just smoking? Yet why stop so close to home, after already having completed the bulk of the journey?

Perhaps he was in conversation with someone? If a sinister fate did befall McLaren, it would explain the missing money, but not how his body washed up in Loch Tay, three quarters of a mile away. To kill McLaren and drag his body as far as the water's edge would require some considerable effort. However, there is no evidence that the body had found its way into the water on that night. Indeed, the earlier searches had yielded nothing in the Loch. Perhaps it was moved, in a panic caused by the presence of search parties, and dumped into the Loch a few days later.

Of the possible explanations, an accident seems the least likely, bearing in mind the distance between the body and the discovered items. Especially as all his possessions were recovered – apart from the pocket-book containing the money. McLaren was not a heavy drinker and was well known to be a man of regular habits.

Did a group of travelling gypsies rob him, perhaps after he turned and made his way back down the hill towards Kenmore? This was a regular occurrence in the area at that time, although it was unusual for travellers to be camping in the hills during the winter months.

There is one further disturbing explanation which was not explored at the time and has only recently come to light. McLaren, 20 years previously, had given evidence in a murder trial, leading to the conviction of a killer. He had been a key witness to a brutal assault on the Fortingall Road. The killer, recently released, and returned to the region, may have spotted McLaren and decided to follow him, or perhaps lay in wait. His family and friends had also sworn revenge at the time of the trial.

Did they argue on the hillside road before extracting a terrible revenge, or did McLaren meet with a freak accident? Without the benefit of forensics and other modern methods, the story will probably always remain a mystery.

# MURDER
## AT CROFTGARROW

On the night of Friday 26th June 1868 an unusual murder took place, on the Fortingall to Kenmore road, which shocked the local community and is, perhaps, linked to another chapter in this book (The Lost Shepherd).

Although more than 150 years have passed since the terrible crime took place, thanks to meticulous records and reporting, the exact spot at which the murder took place is still known, and full transcripts of everything that took place still survive.

Around 9 o'clock in the evening, two men, John McMartin and John McLaren, were travelling in their horse and cart, to share a glass of whisky at the Croftgarrow Inn, on the Fortingall to Kenmore road. After a long hot day, the farm worker and the ploughman were looking forward to a mutchkin (approximately three-quarters of a litre) or two of whisky. They were soon joined by George MacKay, a shepherd from Glenlyon, and James Robertson, a gamekeeper. The four men travelled towards the Inn, however a few hundred yards before they got there, MacKay leapt from the cart, carrying his shepherd's stick, and Robertson also. Shortly afterwards, MacKay entered the Inn. The group already at the Inn asked him if he had misplaced his stick. MacKay claimed he had dropped it outside on the road.

It appeared the shepherd and the farmworker had argued the previous afternoon, after McMartin had accidently touched MacKay with his whip. Evidently the disagreement continued into the next day and the pair 'squared up' at the roadside. MacKay later returned home to the bothy he shared at Glenlyon House with Andrew White, a ploughman. White remembered MacKay coming in, striking a match and looking in the mirror. White remarked to him that there was blood on his face. MacKay immediately went outside and washed his face in the burn at the front of the bothy. On returning inside, he told White that he and McMartin had "bad blood between them" and had come to blows at the roadside.

Shortly afterwards Mrs McMartin (mother of John McMartin) called upon White and MacKay asking for their assistance. Her son was slumped in the roadside, unable to move. The party carried John into the family kitchen and laid him to rest on a barrow. His head was slumped, and first impressions were that he was the worse for drink. However, on removing his clothes, Mrs McMartin noticed two holes in his jacket. On his left side, just below his chest were two wounds, both gurgling with blood. Dr McIntyre was summoned, who in turn summoned the local police. McMartin was made as comfortable as possible and confined to bed. John Allan, the Aberfeldy police sergeant, questioned McMartin on the following afternoon. He was able to answer questions, although obviously weakened. McMartin informed Sergeant Allan that "MacKay did it". MacKay had boasted he could "thrash any man in Perthshire" and, with McMartin on the ground, he had taken out his knife. John McMartin was able to grab MacKay by the wrist, but with his other hand and his teeth, MacKay was able to open the blade and plunge the knife into McMartin's side. McMartin exclaimed "George, you have killed me altogether now". MacKay ignored the cry however and, once more, stabbed the blade into his side. McMartin slumped on the ground, was kicked again in the chest by MacKay, who then left him senseless at the roadside.

John McMartin passed away early on the Monday morning. Following his death bed evidence, Police Sergeant Allan wasted no time in arresting George MacKay, who was charged as follows:

*George MacKay (a shepherd residing at Glenlyon House), you are charged with the crime of murder, in so far as on the night of 26th, or the morning of the 27th day of June, on the public road leading from Fortingall to Kenmore, at a part about 836 yards east from the Public- House at Croftgarrow, occupied by Robert Stewart, publican, you did assault John McMartin, farm servant, son of Archibald McMartin, farmer and miller of Balnald, and did strike him with your fists, and stab him twice on the left side of the chest, with a knife or other sharp instrument, whereby he was mortally wounded.*

A trial date was set for Thursday 17th September 1868, and George MacKay pled not guilty. Despite his previous good record, and several witnesses claimed that MacKay was not "one for the drink", the evidence of McMartin, taken on his death bed, seemed to sway the case in favour of the prosecution. Dr Reid and Dr Absolon, who had performed the autopsy, pointed out that the knife used had entered the body between the fifth and sixth, and ninth and tenth ribs, puncturing the lungs and causing severe loss of blood. There was also a bruise on the chest, corroborating McMartin's story that he had been punched or kicked in the chest.

Perhaps most damning of all was evidence given by Sergeant Allan, in which he detailed the confession MacKay gave during their journey to Perth police station. Sergeant Allan informed the court that MacKay admitted to stabbing McMartin, but claimed he had acted in self-defence, after McMartin had attempted to choke him. This unsubstantiated evidence would, of course, not be permitted in a murder trial today.

In his defence MacKay was only permitted to have a prepared statement read to the court. This was done, on his behalf, by Mr Charles Scott, solicitor from Perth:

*I was going home with John McMartin from Croftgarrow Inn. On the way, McMartin wanted to turn back..... I kept him from going back, but no blows were exchanged. We walked about 50 yards farther when McMartin again struggled to get away, and hit me when I tried to prevent him. He took hold of my tartan neckerchief and I took a large clasp knife out of my pocket to cut the neckerchief, as I was in danger of being choked. At this time we fell to the ground, McMartin's head striking the paling (pointed fence post). McMartin cried and swore, and I was not aware that he had been stabbed. He did not say he was stabbed. We both got up, and as he was threatening me, I ran off and left him and went to my bed.*

Numerous witnesses were produced, all stating that MacKay was a quiet and civil man, trusted and respected and of superior intelligence. Mr Scott, defending, stated that no one, save the dying man, had directly accused MacKay of the crime. Scott also reminded the court that McMartin was very much "the worse for drink", at the time of the altercation, while MacKay was not "under the influence". It was also possible, he added, that McMartin's injuries could have been caused by falling on the fence paling or onto the stony road. He confidently predicted the jury could do nothing other than conclude that his client was not guilty, and that the injuries must have been self-inflicted.

Following the summing up from the Lord Justice Clerk, the Rev Mr Milne, the jury retired to consider their verdict. After just 12 minutes they returned into the hushed Perth Courtroom. The verdict was handed to the Lord Justice Clerk, MacKay was found guilty, by unanimous verdict, not of murder, but of culpable homicide.

He was sentenced to 10 year's penal servitude and removed from the court. MacKay's family members and closest friends shouted loudly from the public gallery, swearing to seek their revenge on those who had "spoke against our George". One of the men they accused was the young ploughman, John McLaren, whose evidence for the prosecution had helped convict MacKay.

McLaren would meet his death in suspicious circumstances, many years later, and that story is dealt with in the chapter *The Lost Shepherd.*

# TWO BODIES, SAME DAY

There are few places in Perthshire more remote than Dalnacardoch, north of Blair Atholl. Yet here, in July 1843, the gruesome discovery of not one, but two bodies were made. Both on the same day.

Dalnacardoch lies in the Glen of Garry, 15 miles northwest of Pitlochry, a tranquil area close to the River. On the orders of King George III, a stagecoach hostelry and inn was built on the site in 1774, for the use of weary travellers on the road north to Inverness. Later, the inn would become a shooting lodge and deer forest.

The forests of Dalnacardoch proved an ideal location for Bonnie Prince Charlie, who sheltered here on the night of 29th August 1745.

On 29th July 1843, still 20 years before the opening of the Highland Railway, the journey north was an arduous one. Work was commissioned to build a new road through a section of land beneath the hills of Drumochter just north of Dalnacardoch. Whilst clearing the roadside, the workmen came across a human skull. Above the left eye, on the temporal bone, the skull bore the unmistakable marks of violence. A large area had been shattered, more than likely by a heavy blow. The men realised immediately that something sinister had taken place and searched the surrounded area. Nearby they discovered, still partially buried, the remains of a human skeleton. The body - that of a man - was doubled up in the foetal position, as if curled up tight in a vain attempt by the victim to shield himself from a fatal blow. It appeared that the body had been in the ground for some time. The only clue to the victim's identity being some decomposed clothing still attached to the right leg.

An investigation by the authorities in Perth noted some other features that suggested a violent death, however these were not made public. The only clue to the victim's identity that could be concluded, was that he was, in all likelihood, a traveller, who had been rumoured locally to have met a violent death a few years previously. Stories had persisted in the area that a vagrant had been beaten to death and his body buried.

If construction on the great road north had not begun, perhaps the mystery would never have been resolved.

If the gruesome unearthing of one body was unlikely, in such a remote district, then the discovery of another body – on the same day – was even more surprising and shocking.

Early in the morning of 29th July, the County police constable in Pitlochry spotted three young men, of shabby appearance, sauntering through the village. There were strangers in the area and his attention was drawn by their suspicious behaviour. He approached them, immediately asking them who they were and their intended destination. The men quickly answered, giving their names, Charles MacDonald, John Jack and Duncan MacCallum, and that they were cotton spinners from Glasgow, on their way to seek work in the mills of Inverness.

Nevertheless, the constable was suspicious of the three men and escorted them to the northerly limit of his district and handed them over to the constable of the next district. He, in turn, did the same until the men reached Dalnacardoch. However shortly afterwards, approximately a mile further along the road, the police constable discovered the body of the youngest of the three men, Duncan MacCallum, lying at the roadside, his body displaying all the characteristics of a vicious assault. The officer quickly summoned help and the small group pursued the remaining two men north on the road, knowing they could not be too far ahead. Within a few miles the men were apprehended

and arrested, then escorted north to Inverness. They
were indicted as followed:

*On the 29th July 1843 the said Charles MacDonald (aged
18) and John Jack (16), on the high road leading from
Dalnacardoch to Dalwhinnie, and a part there of lying
betwixt the march between the counties of Perth and Inverness,
and Dalwhinnie, in the parish of Kingussie, and in the shire
of Inverness, did wickedly and feloniously attack and assault
Duncan MacCallum, then or lately residing in Cannon Street
of Anderston, near Glasgow, and did repeatedly knock him
to the ground, and did, with a leather belt or strap, and with
a stick, and also with their fists and feet, strike him on the
legs and thighs, on the right shoulder, the right arm, on the
right side of the chest, on the wrist, and on other parts of the
body; and did drag him along the said road, and force him
repeatedly into a burn in the neighbourhood of the said road;
and did throw water on him; by all which, all part thereof,
the said Duncan MacCallum was severely bruised and
wounded to the effusion of his blood and serious injury of his
person; and expired in the course of a short time thereafter, on
or near said road, and was thus cruelly murdered.*

MacDonald and Jack pleaded not guilty to the charge.
Three witnesses were produced, who had all seen the
two men beating MacCullum – who was aged only
14, and both the youngest and smallest of the party.
Thomas Smith, a mason, and William Cummings,
a quarrier, and Lachlan MacPhael, a cattle drover,
had seen the boys cruelly beating MacCallum, then
throwing water over him, in an attempt to sober him

up. A further witness, Robert Mackie (a carrier), had passed the group on the road. Mackie noticed the pathetic state of MacCallum. His clothes were in rags and he was barefoot. He was clearly heavily fatigued and unable to continue his journey. MacDonald and Jack, clearly annoyed with their younger companion, had taken to kicking and beating him. Robert Mackie, in an effort to help, gave the group three gills of whisky and continued on his way.

However, an examination of the body, by Dr Murray of Kingussie, and Dr Nicol of Inverness, concluded that the external injuries to the boy were not enough to cause death. This fact shocked the courtroom and led to the charge of murder, and even culpable homicide being dropped. Lord Medwyn dismissed the case, released MacDonald and Jack, even censuring Robert Mackie, the witness, for giving whisky to the group, telling the court that the alcohol had, no doubt, contributed to the boy's death.

In an archetypal example of the Victorian legal system, the presence of strong drink proved, once again, to be a mitigating circumstance used to explain the actions of the accused. In fact, the *Perthshire Courier*, on Thursday 12th October 1843, in their report of the case, made the following comment:

*It is too clear that the unfortunate occurrence was mainly caused by the thoughtlessness of the carrier giving spirits to the boys, and we hope the circumstances will operate as a warning.*

# SCOTLAND'S OLDEST INN

Nestled in the peaceful and picturesque village of Kenmore, sits the Kenmore Hotel. The distinctive black and white building, with its unusual porch and columns created from ancient, blackened tree trunks, has commanded a view across the hills, loch and local community, since its origins in 1502.

The then laird Colin Campbell commissioned the construction of a large hotel and tavern in 1572. His wife and servant were then granted a lease to run an "honest hotel", which has operated ever since.

Yet despite its tranquil and rural setting, the hostelry has witnessed some colourful and tragic events in the 450 years since first opening its doors.

In the summer of 1650 Oliver Cromwell and his troops pursued the Earl of Montrose across Scotland. Buildings in the area were torched and locals feared reprisals from the English army, unless they appeared sympathetic to Cromwell and his men. The Kenmore Hotel "welcomed" and served Cromwell and his officers with a hearty supper. If the meal and the hospitality had not proved satisfactory, then the hotel would have been razed to the ground, making its story a comparatively short one!

In 1787 the poet Robert "Rabbie" Burns visited the hotel and – struck by the beauty of the village – inscribed in pencil a poem on the chimney breast of the parlour at the inn.

*"Admiring Nature in her wildest grace,*
*These northern scenes with weary feet I trace"*

Burns was followed by a William Wordsworth, who also visited the hotel, and by Queen Victoria and Prince Albert, who honeymooned there. The poem by Burns is still visible in the bar of the Kenmore Hotel, providing a romantic glimpse into its past. However, other events in the hotel's annals paint a very different picture.

On the evening of Monday 30th June 1834, following the market, the hotel was busier than usual, and the bar was packed. Large amounts of whisky were consumed and John Walker, the innkeeper, and his staff were kept busy dealing with the throng of rowdy customers.

A local stonemason, Donald McNaughton, had been drinking heavily and had become more and more rowdy. He attempted to go up the stairs towards the dining room, but in his drunken state blocked the stairway, at the dogleg, and clashed with James Menzies, one of the hotel's waiters. McNaughton and Menzies argued, a scuffle ensuing and both parties raised their hands to each other. Menzies apparently pushed McNaughton along the dogleg in the stairs, as he attempted to pass him. What happened next is unclear. The intoxicated McNaughton backed himself into a corner, on the bend in the stairs, and Menzies possibly grabbed him by the collar. The waiter, Menzies, was clearly angry at this point (as later described by a witness), however whether Donald McNaughton fell or was pushed is uncertain. What is known though, is that McNaughton fell backwards down the eight steps, probably smashing his head on the stone floor at the bottom. His legs were slumped on the first two treads, his unmoving head and shoulders left resting on the hard floor. Two witnesses, Duncan Anderson and John Campbell, both working at the hotel on that evening, overheard the argument between Menzies and McNaughton on the stair, although neither saw the actual fall. Both did later testify in court that the two men had argued, and that Menzies seemed to be very angry. Neither witness could be sure that Menzies had watched McNaughton fall down the stairs or was simply unaware.

Donald McNaughton, prostrate and senseless, at the foot of the stairs, was carried through to the hotel kitchen and laid out on a bed of straw. Dr Peter MacGillewie (a surgeon) examined McNaughton but could not detect any marks of violence on the body. He visited him again at 10am the following morning and discovered McNaughton still senseless. Shortly after the doctor's departure, around noon, McNaughton passed away. His body was buried soon after. However, a more detailed study into the events of that night and the contradictory evidence of the witnesses led to further investigations. It was claimed, by one witness, Menzies may have grabbed McNaughton by the wrists and pushed him down the stairs. However, another witness thought Menzies may have simply brushed the drunken McNaughton aside, while on his way to the dining room, and been completely unaware of his fall.

Nevertheless, the body was exhumed several weeks later and examined by Dr Malcolm and again by Dr MacGillewie. A fracture of the cranium was discovered, which would have undoubtedly resulted in death. This would not have been detected by Dr MacGillewie on the night of the incident, probably due to the poor lighting available and the fact that the surface of the skin had not been broken and "the bone not laid bare".

Dr Malcolm reported his findings as follows:

*"The injury on the skull was of such a nature as to occasion death; we do not think that a fall on a wooden stair would cause such a fracture; there were five steps, and he must have fallen backwards with considerable violence on the stone flat at the bottom, to cause such a fracture."*

James Menzies was arrested and charged with culpable homicide:

*"James Menzies, waiter in the employment of John Walker, innkeeper at the Kenmore Hotel, is accused of culpable homicide, on the 30th June last, he did at the same inn attack and assault the now deceased Donald McNaughton, mason at Rievuckie, in the Parish of Kenmore, and did push him down a stair whereby he sustained such injuries as occasioned his death next day."*

Menzies entered a plea of not guilty at his trial in October 1834. His defence was passionately argued by Perth solicitor Mr Patton, who called several witnesses from the hotel. Each spoke of James Menzies's character and his quiet nature. The intoxicated condition of Donald McNaughton also gave credence to the possibility of the fall being accidental. Following an expert summing up by Lord Medwyn, the jury retired. After half an hour a verdict of 'Not Proven' was returned and James Menzies walked free from the courtroom.

****

Monday 30th September 1901 was a pleasant autumn evening in Kenmore. At approximately 9pm a handsome young man, aged about 27, entered the Kenmore Hotel. He was around 5 feet 8 inches in height, with curly brown hair and a pleasant manner and appearance. The waiter engaged in casual conversation with the stranger:

"Where have you come from, sir?"

"I have just arrived from Tarbet, Loch Lomond", came the reply.

The waiter, thinking it odd, suggested to the visitor, "But, you could not have come by boat or by coach at this time?"

The stranger admitted this and replied; "Yes, I have walked."

The answer seemed odd, Tarbet being some 50 miles from Kenmore, and the visitor's appearance immaculate. Nothing further was said and the young man took supper in the coffee room, before retiring to his bedroom. He had not signed the visitors' book on arrival and enquired if would be acceptable to sign it in the morning, as the hour was already late. Mr Knight, the son of the proprietor, said this would be perfectly acceptable and wished the new guest "goodnight".

At 9am on the following morning the mysterious guest appeared at breakfast. He seemed to be in good spirits and engaged in conversation with the waiters. Appearing to be a man of culture, he spoke fluently in English, French and German to the staff and other guests in the restaurant. He stated how much he was enjoying the magnificent scenery of the district. Following his hearty breakfast, he was presented with his bill and asked to sign the visitors' book. He apologised and told the waiter;

"I have no money till my luggage comes with the boat from Tarbet at 12.10", he explained, "I will settle up when the steamer arrives."

"That will be alright", replied the waiter.

The stranger then left his key at reception and walked across the square into the Kenmore Post Office, where he wrote two telegrams, one of which was to the Tarbert Hotel, Loch Lomond. This telegram requested that his luggage might be forwarded to Kenmore. However, instead of passing the telegrams over the post office counter, he thrust them into his pocket, unsent, and returned to the hotel.

On reaching the hotel, he requested his key from reception. He was told, however, that his room was being put in order and would he mind waiting for a little while. He replied that this was "absolutely fine" and wandered through to the billiard room. From there, he excused himself and visited the gentleman's lavatories. It was approximately 10am.

Suddenly the sound of a gunshot echoed around the ground floor of the hotel. Startled by the noise,

both guests and staff looked anxiously about. The
same waiter who had served the mysterious visitor
at breakfast opened the door which led into the
gentleman's lavatories. He immediately saw a still-
smoking revolver on the floor. The body of the man
was slumped next to it. The stranger had carefully
removed his collar, shirt, tie and vest before carefully
placing the revolver against his bare breast and firing,
once, into his chest.

The body was removed and stored at the rear of the
hotel while an investigation was undertaken into the
mysterious and enigmatic man. The police examined
the revolver and the man's clothing carefully. The gun,
it seemed, was new yet no trace of ownership or receipt
could be traced. One chamber had been fired, three
were still full and one was left blank. There were 20
spare cartridges in the stranger's pockets, the unsent
telegrams, some loose change and a watch chain, but
no watch. The pockets did not contain any addressed
envelopes, identity of any kind, wallet or letters. In an
inside pocket were discovered some old, used tramway
tickets from London, Liverpool and Glasgow.

The police conducted extensive enquires, both in the
Kenmore and Aberfeldy area, as well as in Tarbert. No
luggage ever arrived on the 12.10 steamer from Tarbet
that morning and enquires at the Tarbet Hotel in Loch
Lomond revealed no missing guest, or any outstanding
luggage due to be sent on to Kenmore.  Information
was provided to several Scottish newspapers but failed
to produce a clue to the man's identity. Enquires in

Tarbet yielded nothing and no one matching the man's description was reported missing.

Several witnesses in Aberfeldy did report seeing a man, matching the description given, in the town on the previous evening. He had caught the eye of passers-by, due to his distinctive cycling shoes. However, attempts to trace this man also proved fruitless.

Following a full investigation, it was determined that the young man had lost all his money and decided to take his own life in a quiet and out of the way place. After three months the enquiry was wound down. The mystery of the well-spoken man who claimed to have travelled from Tarbet was never solved. His remains were never identified, and his body never claimed.

**\*\*\*\***

Surprisingly, for such a quiet and tranquil setting, the tragic suicide of the unknown man in 1901 is not the only case of a gun being fired inside the Kenmore Hotel.

Following events that took place on Saturday 30th May 1908 a charge of "reckless discharge of a firearm" was brought against William Morris, a miller from Acharn, after he fired his pistol within the taproom of the hotel, narrowly missing Alexander McLaren, a labourer from Styx.

The room (known locally as room number 3) had been busy that evening and several witnesses noticed Morris holding a pistol on his left side. He appeared to be ramming something into the muzzle of the gun.

The witnesses John McGregor, Alexander McLaren and Alexander McIntosh all asked McLaren to put away his pistol. McLaren appeared to do so, however shortly afterwards he was seen holding the pistol again and a shot rang out.

The bullet narrowly missed Alexander McLaren, who initially thought it had hit him on the cheek. Those present in the taproom were visibly shaken and the hotel keeper, Mr Currie, summoned the police who arrested William Morris. He was charged with the "reckless discharge of a firearm" and pled not guilty.

Once again, a case involving the Kenmore Hotel saw a court trial and widespread newspaper coverage. On this occasion, however, William Morris was able to persuade the court that the gun was purely used for bird scaring and that it had discharged accidently. On leaving the Kenmore Hotel, on the evening of the incident, he had thrown the pistol into Loch Tay. Without the gun to check, the court had little evidence on which to base a verdict. Morris was fined £3 (approximately £350 today) and warned over his future behaviour.

It is interesting to note that the oldest hotel in Scotland, now famed for its peaceful Highland location, desirability as a wedding venue, and for salmon fishing, holds many colourful secrets in its long and interesting history.

# THE CROWN HOTEL SHOOTING

Shortly after 7pm on Sunday 6th May 1951 the muffled sound of two gunshots could be heard in Bank Street, Aberfeldy. Passers by stopped, looked around, not entirely sure from which direction the shots had emanated. As the sequence of events unravelled, the full details would emerge of a tragedy that shocked the peaceful post-war community and attracted nationwide attention.

Walter Jamieson, who had celebrated his 21st birthday just three days earlier, was engaged as porter (affectionately known as "Boots") at The Crown Hotel in Bank Street, Aberfeldy on Friday 4th May. Originally from Dundee, he had previously worked at the Breadalbane Arms Hotel, after leaving his apprenticeship as a butcher.

It had been a busy Sunday and the hotel staff were not able to tackle the washing up until 6pm. Jamieson, and the three waitresses, Margaret Munro, Margaret McAspurren and Margaret Douthwaite, settled down to the arduous task. An hour later, after stepping

outside for some fresh air and a cigarette, the girls
suggested making a cup of tea in the kitchen. Jamieson
joined them. Margaret Munro asked Jamieson to fetch
some milk from the pantry, while the girls all went to
the toilet. Unknown to Jamieson, Margaret Munro had
planned a small prank at Jamieson's expense. "We'll
lock him in the pantry for a laugh" she whispered to
the others. As Jamieson passed through the door into
the pantry, Margaret Munro quickly pulled the door
shut and turned the key in the lock. The girls then left
the kitchen, giggling to themselves.

Walter Jamieson, realising exactly what had happened,
panicked, and reached for the shotgun (which was
propped against the wall of the pantry). He fired one
.22 cartridge through the door of the pantry, into the
wall of the empty kitchen beyond. The door was of
a double plywood construction, but did little to slow
down the velocity of the bullet. Jamieson then stepped
to the back of the pantry, threw the empty cartridge
out of the pantry window and reloaded. Apparently
unknown to Jamieson, the girls, still laughing to
themselves, had tiptoed back into the kitchen.

Jamieson, holding the gun at hip height, fired
another shot through the still locked pantry door.
The bullet grazed the scalp of Margaret McAspurren
and struck Margaret Munro flush in the temple. She
collapsed immediately to the floor.

Screaming, the girls unlocked the pantry door and cried out: "What have you done? You've hurt her Walter." Initially they were unsure if Margaret Munro was seriously hurt, until they noticed the blood oozing from the wound. "It was an accident", Jamieson cried out.

Dr Swanson was called, and he rushed to the hotel. Margaret Munro's mother was also sent for, from the family home, just 200 yards away in Kenmore Street. Walter Jamieson also collapsed, apparently suffering from shock, and both were taken to the Cottage Hospital in Aberfeldy.

Margaret Munro passed away within a few minutes. Aged just 20, she had worked at The Crown Hotel since leaving Breadalbane Academy in the town. Jamieson, visibly shocked and shaking, was arrested at the Cottage Hospital and charged with culpable homicide.

He was escorted to Perth but released on bail at a cost of £12.

Under expert guidance in court from Mr AF Steele, a Perth solicitor, Jamieson pleaded guilty to a charge of recklessly discharging a shotgun. The charge of culpable homicide was dropped. Mr Steele was able to gain the sympathy of the court with a thorough defence. Jamieson was examined by a psychiatrist, who gave evidence stating that Jamieson was "more likely than the average person to respond hysterically to being locked in a room", due to his childhood experiences. Jamieson recalled, from the age of 10, being locked in a room by his mother. In desperation he would beat on the door. His calls would go unheeded until he eventually cried himself to sleep. Later his parents divorced, and he chose to live with his father, who died shortly afterwards. Jamieson was then taken in by his landlady. He joined the RAF, but was discharged after just 12 weeks, due to ill health. With no other relatives in Dundee (his family being originally from Aberdeen), he had eventually migrated to the Aberfeldy area.

Jamieson's condition and past were taken into account by Sheriff Prain, however the act of discharging the shotgun was described in court as "a most gross and reckless act with very serious consequences". He was sentenced to six months imprisonment.

Margaret Munro was buried locally, and the town grieved.

Walter Jamieson, after release from prison, eventually moved to the Aberdeen area. In a strange twist of fate, eight years later in 1960, he was to save the life of a baby trapped in burning bedroom. He was returning home, with his wife Gladys from an evening stroll in Powis Circle, Aberdeen. Nearing home, they noticed smoke belching from their neighbour's windows, coupled with the terrifying sound of children screaming. Jamieson described his actions as follows:

"I immediately dashed out and phoned the fire brigade. I came back and had to smash one of the panes in the front bedroom window. I managed to climb up and look in the window, but the smoke was so thick I couldn't see anything.

I knew there was somebody in the house as I heard screaming. I ran to the back of the house and got in by the scullery door. I saw the baby, June, in her pram. There were flames behind the door. I snatched up the baby. I then went to the lobby and got the other children out by the door."

The children had been alone in the house at the time.

Perhaps the tragic experience in Aberfeldy had strengthened his resolve? Had he not been determined to make amends, perhaps he would not have been able to enter the burning building. His fear of confined spaces would have undoubtedly made the rescue attempt harder. It is not known if his wife knew of his previous misdemeanour, however from one tragic mistake, a hero did, at least, emerge.

# ACKNOWLEDGEMENTS
## AND REFERENCES

This book would not have been possible without the encouragement and support of Kevin and Jayne Ramage and The Watermill Bookshop in Aberfeldy. Thank you for your patience, kind words and guidance. I would also like to express my gratitude to the Aberfeldy Community Library, Pitlochry & Moulin Heritage Centre, Perth & Kinross Council Archives, Elaine Dunsmore, Ellen McBride, and to all the family and friends that have encouraged my endeavours.

The following sources of information have also been invaluable in either helping to piece together the stories contained in this book, or for kindly supplying their permission for the reproduction of images and text:

Aberfeldy Community Library, Aberfeldy Museum, Kenmore Hotel, Pitlochry & Moulin Heritage Centre, Perth & Kinross Council Archives, Perth Sheriff's Court

*Aberfeldy Past & Present* by Neil MacKay, *Whisky Wars* by Malcolm Archibald, *Visions of Britain*

British Civil War Trust, The Robert Burns Society, Office for National Statistics, Ordnance Survey

British Newspaper Archive and the following newspapers and journals:

*The Press & Journal, Evening Telegraph, Dundee Courier, Perthshire Advertiser, The Belfast Newletter, The Evening Post, The Fife Free Press, The Kirkintilloch Gazette, The Scotsman, Sunday Post, The Mercury, Western Morning News, Leeds Times, The South London Press, Oban Times, The Ipswich Journal, The Alloa Advertiser, The Paisley Herald, The Berkshire Chronicle, Montrose, Arbroath & Brechin Review, The Citizen, The Standard, Evening Express, Daily Record, Aberdeen Weekly Journal, The Southern Reporter, London Gazette, The Heartlander Magazine*

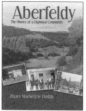